Mayan Calendar Prophecies:
Predictions for 2012-2052

What the Mayan Civilization's History & Mythology Can Tell Us About Our Future

Gary C. Daniels

Mayan Calendar Prophecies: Predictions for 2012-2052

© 2012 Gary C. Daniels

Visit me at:

www.TheRealMayanProphecies.com

www.LostWorlds.org

www.Facebook.com/lostworlds

All rights reserved. No part of this publication may be reproduced, stored in a retrieval system, or transmitted in any way or by any means, electronic, mechanical, photocopying, recording or otherwise, without the prior written permission of the copyright holder.

PICTURE ACKNOWLEDGEMENTS

Cover Images:

Cover Artwork by Victor Habbick

Earth, Galaxy, Sun by NASA.

Cover Design by Gary C. Daniels.

ISBN-13: 978-1480032583
ISBN-10: 1480032581

**For my wife, Lina, and daughter, Savannah.
May our future be bright.**

Table of Contents

I. Background 7
1. Prophecy...or Predictions? 8
2. The Mayan Calendar Cycles 11
3. The Science of Cycles 13

II. The Katun Prophecies 21
4. Predictions for Katun 4 Ahau (1993-2012) 22
5. Predictions for Katun 2 Ahau (2012-2032) 35
6. Predictions for Katun 13 Ahau (2032-2052) 40

III. Beyond 2012 49
7. Quest for the Truth about 2012 and Beyond 50
8. Comet Machholz and the Return of Kukulkan 53
9. Prelude to Disaster? 61
10. Quetzalcoatl & Hermes: Cosmic Messengers? 68
11. Younger Dryas Climate Event & the Clovis Comet 75
12. Super Solar Flares 77
13. Thoth, the Egyptian Messenger of the Sun God................79
14. The Galactic Center and the Blue Star Kachina 85

IV. What Happened the Last Time the Calendar Ended? . 89
15. Decoding the Mayan Flood Myth 90
    What was the cosmic crocodile? 92
    What was the flood of blood? 95
    Mayan flood caused by impact mega-tsunami? 98
    A Cycle of Cosmic Catastrophes? 102
    Supernova or Galactic Core Explosion? 104
    Yax Naah Itzamnaaj & the Constellation Draco....................107
    Conclusions 109
16. Decoding the Mayan Blowgunner Vase...........................110

V. Comet Catastrophe 117
17. Rahu and Ketu: A Hindu Account....................................118
18. Samson: A Biblical Account...127
19. Medusa: A Greek Account 131
20. Taotie: A Chinese Account...140
21. The Other Legend of Kukulkan & the True Origins of the Mayan Calendar 147

VI. The 2012 Prophecy.. 155

 21. Decoding the Aztec Calendar Stone 156
 22. Decoding Tortuguero's Monument 6 169
 23. End of the Cycle 175

VII. The End 179
 24. Conclusion 180

Afterword 183

Author's Note 185

Appendices 187
 A. Witches, Dragons, Halloween & Christmas 189
 B. Creation Story from the Chilam Balam of Chumayel 196
  Chapter X. The Creation of the World 196
 C. The Katun Prophecies from the Chilam Balam of
 Chumayel 203
  Chapter XVIII A Series of Katun Prophecies 204
  Chapter XXII A Book of Katun Prophecies 206
  Chapter XXIV Prophecies of a New Religion 209
 D. The Mayan Chronicles from the Chilam Balam of
 Chumayel 212
  Chapter XIX The First Chronicle 212
  Chapter XX The Second Chronicle 214
  Chapter XXI The Third Chronicle 216

References 219
About the Author 239

I. Background

1. Prophecy…or Predictions?

What is the difference between a prophecy and a prediction? A prophecy is usually the result of some type of vision or divine intervention received by a spiritual specialist like a shaman or priest. A prediction, on the other hand, can be made by anyone through careful observations that lead to the detection of a pattern. Meteorologists make predictions every night on your local news based not on divine intervention but by careful observation of data and then applying their knowledge of weather patterns to this data to predict what may happen next.

As Mayan scholar David Stuart noted in his book *The Order of Days: The Mayan World and the Truth About 2012*, the Mayan prophetic books known as *Chilam Balam* utilized past events to predict future events. He noted that Mayan "prophets" did not simply receive visions and make random predictions. Instead they created a careful analytical system that looked for patterns in past historical events that took place in previous periods called *katuns* and then from these tried to make projections into the future. In fact, this analytical system sounds very similar to modern scientific forecasting.

The book you are reading now is based on the idea that the Maya made predictions, not prophecies, based on careful observations of patterns including astronomical cycles as well as historical cycles of civilization. Just as human beings follow a predictable pattern of development from fetal development through childhood, adolescence and adulthood so, perhaps, do civilizations follow predictable patterns of development and collapse.

Pick up any book on childhood development and you will find precise, to the month, predictions of when certain milestones will be achieved. As a new father I have been continually amazed at how accurate such books have been in alerting me to each new phase of my daughter's development! Yet I do not think the authors were endowed with divine insights and the gift of prophecy. They are simply relating normal cycles of human development arrived at through careful observation. Thus the

Maya likely discovered a similar predictable pattern of development for civilizations that they recorded in their "prophetic" books.

Years before I researched the ancient Maya and became aware of their 256-year *katun* cycle, I accidentally discovered a similar 250-year cycle relating to the rise and fall of Native American civilizations. I noted on my website LostWorlds.org that it appeared many Native American settlements lasted for around 250 years before being abandoned or destroyed. I theorized that this was likely the length of time required for a settlement to grow to a size that would either exhaust its local resources or encroach on surrounding settlements and cause conflict. Thus when I discovered that the Maya believed in a 256-year cycle related to the rise and fall of civilizations, I immediately became intrigued.

The study of cycles is nothing new. In fact, in 1931 the U.S. government through the Department of Commerce commissioned a task force headed by Harvard economist Edward Dewey to discover the underlying dynamics of the Great Depression. Dewey combined enormous research in business cycles with research from leading biologists on cycles in nature and in wildlife. He was astonished to discover that cycles of identical length were found in both disciplines and similar cycles from different areas reached their peaks and troughs at the same time.[1] This led Dewey to devote his life to cycle research and founded the Foundation for the Study of Cycles which still conducts research today across all scientific disciplines.

Dewey stated in 1967:

"Cycles are meaningful, and all science that has been developed in the absence of cycle knowledge is inadequate and partial. ...any theory of economics, sociology, history, medicine, or climatology that ignores non-chance rhythms is as manifestly incomplete as medicine was before the discovery of germs."[2]

Thus the idea that cycles do, in fact, exist and they can

predict the rise and fall of everything from wheat prices to human civilization is founded in science. Thus it would be wise not to completely dismiss the Mayan "prophecies" or predictions out-of-hand as mere superstitious nonsense. (I will discuss more of the science behind cycles in Chapter 3.)

Is there anything to the Mayan predictions and forecasts as written in the books of *Chilam Balam*? This book was created to explore that very idea. There are primarily two types of 2012 books and websites: "true believers" and "debunkers." And both types are hyper-focused on a single date: December 21, 2012. Yet the Maya conception of time was both linear **and** cyclical thus 2012 was simultaneously the ending of one cycle and the beginning of another and just one stop on a timeline that stretched into the future without end. Likewise, the predictions in the *Chilam Balam* are not focused on this single date and can be used to make forecasts and predictions for dates far beyond 2012.

This book offers a third approach, neither "true believer" nor "debunker," instead I will approach this subject the way an ancient Mayan priest would by looking at past events and comparing them to present-day realities in order to create the most probable scenarios and forecasts for the future. I present the latest news and scientific research to see how well these correspond to the Mayan conception of the qualities of each *katun* period. Just like the ancient Maya, I will study past events and try to determine patterns from which I can extrapolate possible future scenarios that are consistent with the Mayan *katun* prophecies. I will also explore Mayan history and mythology to see how they might influence these predictions and future scenarios. Armed with this information, you can draw your own conclusions about the Mayan calendar and its predictions for 2012 and beyond.

2. The Mayan Calendar Cycles

Did the Maya really predict the end of the world on December 21, 2012? If not, then what *did* the Maya actually predict for 2012?

The ancient Maya believed that civilizations went through predictable cycles. These cycles repeated every 256 years. This 256-year cycle could be broken down into thirteen 19.7-year periods (19.7 x 13 = 256) called *katuns*. Each *katun* had a name and was associated with a particular prophecy or prediction. These predictions were recorded in their prophetic books known as the *Chilam Balam*. (The image below is a page from one such book illustrating the thirteen *katun* cycles.)

Above: Copy of the Book of Chilam Balam of Ixil displayed at the Museo Nacional de Anthropologia in Mexico-City. Photo by Carlos Reusser Monsalvez.

For instance, according to the Maya we currently live in the cycle named *Katun 4 Ahau* that began in 1993 and ends in 2012. The cycle that begins in 2012 is named *Katun 2 Ahau* and ends in 2032. The next cycle is named *Katun 13 Ahau* and runs until 2052 and is the final *katun* in the present 256-year cycle that began in 1796. The *katun* cycle then begins again in 2052 with *Katun 11 Ahau*. (The predictions associated with these *katuns* will be discussed in Section II: The Katun Prophecies.)

The first question you might have is, "I thought the Mayan calendar ended on December 21, 2012 not in 2052?" The Maya had multiple calendars. The calendar that "ends" on December 21,

2012 is called the Long Count calendar. It consists of 13 *baktuns*. One *baktun* equals 20 *katuns* or 394 years. Thirteen *baktuns* equal 5125 years. The Long Count calendar has a "start date" of August 11, 3114 BC, which the Maya recorded as 13.0.0.0.0, and an "end date" of December 21, 2012.

Curiously, December 21, 2012 is also recorded as 13.0.0.0.0. How can this be? This is because the calendar "rolls over" like an odometer back to 1 after 13.0.0.0.0. For instance, the second day of the Long Count calendar, August 12, 3114 BC, was recorded as 0.0.0.0.1. The calendar will finally reach 13.0.0.0.0 again on December 21, 2012. Thus December 21, 2012 is the "completion" of 13 *baktuns* but it is not the "end" of the calendar. The calendar will once again roll over. (There is only one prophecy associated with this auspicious date. We will explore this prophecy in great detail in Section VI.)

The Mayan *katun* prophecies recorded in the books of *Chilam Balam* are based on the Short Count calendar. The Short Count calendar consists of 13 *katuns* that total 256 years. The Short Count ends on *Katun 13 Ahau* then starts over. As you can see, the number 13 was important to the ancient Maya. This is because the number 13 represented "completion." This is why the Long Count calendar reaching the 13th *baktun* on December 21, 2012 is seen as the "completion" or "end" of the current Long Count calendar cycle.

The current Short Count calendar is out-of-sync with the Long Count and does not end on December 21, 2012 but instead in 2052, forty years later. This suggests that the world will not self-destruct on 12-21-12 as has been popularized in our sensationalist news media. So what exactly *did* the Maya predict for the future and is there any truth behind their belief in repeating cycles?

3. The Science of Cycles

As noted in the previous chapters, the Maya believed a 256-year cycle governed civilizations. Interestingly, scientists have discovered a seismic cycle lasting 250 years,[3] a solar cycle that lasts approximately 250 years,[4] and an ~300-year cycle of impact events on Earth.[5] Could there be any connection between these 250-year cycles and the 256-year *Katun* cycle?

It does not take much imagination to see the connection between seismic activity and the downfall of civilizations. Not only do earthquakes destroy the physical infrastructure of civilizations but they can also produce other effects. Earthquakes can cause volcanic eruptions by destabilizing the volcanic cone. This results in a collapse of the volcano that releases built up pressure resulting in an eruption. This is exactly what occurred at Mount St. Helens in the state of Washington in 1980.

Earthquakes can also trigger massive tsunamis like the Indonesian and Japanese earthquakes in 2004 and 2011. Thus there is a clear cause-and-effect between earthquakes and the downfall of small-scale civilizations that is easy to see.

Probably the most shocking cycle is the recent discovery that the Earth experiences impact events large enough to wipe out a large metropolitan area much more frequently than originally believed perhaps as often as every 300 years. This research concluded, "based on various strands of evidence (for example, the number of meteorites discovered on earth that originated on the moon) that the average time between impacts on earth is no more than 300 years, probably less."[6] The fact that scientists estimate this cycle could be somewhat less then 300 years leaves one question: could it actually be a 256-year cycle?

Three such impact events happened within the twentieth century alone. The most famous of these was the Tunguska event wherein a small comet or comet fragment exploded in the atmosphere over Russian Siberia with an explosive power equal to a nuclear bomb 1,000 times more powerful than the one dropped on Hiroshima, Japan.[7] This explosion flattened trees over an area of 830 square miles. (Eyewitness accounts of this event will be discussed in Chapter 15 "Decoding the Mayan Flood Myth.") The same event happening over any major metropolitan area today would kill millions and be devastating to the region.

Both the seismic cycle and impact cycle offer clear cause-and-effect relationships between cyclical events and the downfall of small-scale civilizations. But how could the solar cycle be associated with the rise and fall of civilizations?

One possible connection between solar cycles and the rise and fall of civilizations is the effect the sun has on climate and precipitation. For instance, one researcher found that Iron Age settlements expanded during periods of high solar activity.[8] This was believed to have been the result of changing levels of rainfall caused by variations in solar output. As rainfall increased these Iron Age settlements could grow and expand. When rainfall decreased and droughts occurred these settlements would naturally contract again. Interestingly, the highest levels of activity in these settlements were recorded between 700-450 BC and 300-50 BC. Each of these time periods lasted exactly 250 years.

A link between disease outbreaks and solar cycles has also recently been discovered that could offer another possible connection between solar cycles and the downfall of civilizations. It was found that pandemic outbreaks of Influenza A only occurred during periods of increased solar activity.[9] This was initially hypothesized to have resulted from solar-induced climate change which altered the arrival times of disease-carrying birds.[10] Later research showed it was more likely related to biological vitamin D production that fluctuated with solar activity.[11]

Vitamin D is primarily produced in humans from exposure to sunlight. Research has noted that vitamin D has been shown to generate positive responses in "the immune, cardio-vascular, muscle, pancreas, and brain systems, as well as positive involvement in ageing and control of the cell cycle and thus of cancer disease process."[12] Production of vitamin D was shown to be highest during periods of *decreased* solar activity and lowest during periods of *increased* solar activity. Thus during increased solar activity the body, due to this lack of vitamin D production, was especially susceptible to infections such as Influenza A. It is likely other diseases would increase similarly due to the same effects.

(Solar activity should not be confused with sunlight. Solar activity refers to the magnetic cycles of the Sun which result in sunspots and solar flares. Increased solar activity *decreases* vitamin D production whereas increased exposure to sunlight *increases* vitamin D production. This is also why more people catch colds during Winter than other times since sunlight exposure is decreased due to the shorter days.)

Other recent research has shown a connection between solar cycles and the human brain including both mental diseases and creativity. The researchers noted that people born during "radiation peaks in solar cycles…[were] associated with a higher incidence of mental disorders, suggesting the sensitivity of ectodermal embryonic tissues to UVR [ultraviolet radiation.]"[13] Other research noted that an increase in first admissions to a psychiatric hospital were associated with increased solar activity.[14] (Perhaps this was due to hallucinations, which appear to increase due to solar activity as well.[15]) Still other research showed bursts of human creativity were strongly correlated with solar cycles.[16] As history has shown it only takes one madman or one genius to cause a civilization to reach new lows or new highs. Thus the Sun could be playing a decisive role in this process.

Russian researcher A. L. Chizhevsky found many more links between human civilization and solar cycles. He found that solar cycles were associated with insect infestations as well as disease epidemics. Insect infestations can, of course, lead to famines and disease outbreaks can likewise bring a civilization to its knees. But these were not the only solar connections Chizhevsky found to the rise and fall of civilizations. According to Wikipedia:

> *"Chizhevsky proposed that not only did geomagnetic storms resulting from sunspot-related solar flares affect electrical usage, plane crashes, epidemics and grasshopper infestations, but human mental life and activity. Increased negative ionization in the atmosphere increased human mass excitability. Chizhevsky proposed that human history is influenced by the eleven year peaks in sunspot activity, triggering humans en masse to act upon existing grievances and complaints through revolts, revolutions, civil wars and wars between nations."*[17]

Thus even human warfare appears to be influenced by solar cycles.

The preceding examples make logical connections between solar cycles, disease outbreaks, insect infestations, rainfall patterns, and mental health (both positive and negative), all of which can have impacts on the rise and fall of civilizations. Yet economists have also noted a connection between stock prices and celestial cycles that do not have such logical, clear-cut, cause-and-effect explanations.

Much research has been conducted trying to find a link between solar cycles and the stock market without success. Yet one line of research found statistically significant correlations between stock prices and, of all things, planetary alignments. Stranger still, these correlations seemed strongest when the planetary alignments occurred while also aligned with the galactic center of our Milky Way galaxy.

Edward Dewey, founder of the Foundation for the Study of Cycles noted in 1969:

> *"since 1897 there has been a correspondence between stock price movements and the times of conjunctions and oppositions of certain planets (the ones nearest the sun) when these conjunctions and oppositions took place in a certain direction in space."*[18]

He noted that stock prices usually moved up, 92% of the time, when the planets were aligned near the galactic center where the Celestial Equator intersected the Galactic Equator. Dewey stated,

> *"The consistency with which stock prices tend to advance during the 30 days prior to conjunctions or oppositions of Mars, and Jupiter, and the superior and inferior conjunctions of Mercury, when in the same segment of space, is truly remarkable, and is surely not chance."*

The cause of such correlations is still unknown but, as will be seen later, this will not be the only connection between the galactic center and events here on earth. What we do know is that the galactic center emits gamma ray radiation.[19] Since stock prices are ultimately the result of human sentiment perhaps the galactic center gamma ray source has cycles that influence the human psyche in ways similar to the previously discussed solar cycles.

The planetary alignments would thus not be the *cause* of the stock price increases but would simply serve like the hands on a clock with their celestial positions coinciding with these galactic center influences and associated stock price movements. Just as the hands on a clock do not cause the sun to move across the sky they just coincide with the daily solar cycle allowing us to know where the sun currently is on its path so too might the positions of the planets let us know "what time it is" in regards to galactic cycles.

It should be noted that all of the above discoveries were made possible by analyzing large data sets. In other words, all one needs to discover such cycles are large sets of accurate, time-based records with which to cross-reference and find correlations. Did the Maya have such records?

Since most Mayan books were burned by Spanish priests, we will never know for sure. The Mayan books that *do* remain show they did, in fact, keep detailed chronicles of events in their history. (See Appendix D.) They also kept detailed records of astronomical observations. Did they also keep sunspot records? Many cultures made sunspot observations throughout history thus an astronomically sophisticated culture like the Maya undoubtedly did so as well. By comparing patterns in their astronomical data with patterns in their historical chronicles did the Maya make similar discoveries a thousand years ago as those we have only made in the past one hundred years?

As we will see in Chapter 16, "Decoding the Mayan Flood Myth," the Maya do seem to have had accurate chronologies dating back at least 5,000 years. This is proven by the fact that they recorded the exact date of a series of catastrophic events near the end of their last calendar cycle.

Evidence proving that such events actually occurred has been discovered in the geologic and Antarctic ice core records corresponding to this same date.

Clearly this is no coincidence. The Maya did not simply get lucky and described events for a random date from 5,000 years ago that researchers would corroborate in the 20th century. The simplest explanation is that the Maya did, in fact, have detailed and dated historical chronologies going back thousands of years. Access to such a large set of data would have undoubtedly given them the ability to detect patterns that even our scientists today are unaware of. More evidence of the existence of these ancient records will be explored in Sections III and IV and the surprising origins of these records as well as their calendar will be discussed in chapter 21.

With this knowledge of cycle science let us now take a look at the actual Mayan prophecies from the past and see what they might predict about the future.

II. The Katun Prophecies

4. Predictions for Katun 4 Ahau (1993-2012)

As stated previously, the primary Mayan prophecies or predictions for 2012 (or any other date) can be found in their books called the *Chilam Balam*. According to their *katun* cycles, we presently live in the cycle named *Katun 4 Ahau*. This cycle began on April 6, 1993 and ends on December 21, 2012. What predictions did the Maya make for this cycle?

There are currently nine known books of *Chilam Balam*. Each contains basically the same predictions with minor variations. I will use a combination of the *Chilam Balam of Chumayel, Codex Perez, and Chilam Balam of Tizim* as the source for this book. According to these sources, the prophecies or predictions for our current cycle, *Katun 4 Ahau*, that began on 4/6/1993 and ends on 12/21/2012 are as follows:

> *This is the katun for remembering knowledge and recording it.*[20]
>
> *"The quetzal shall come, the green bird shall come. Ah Kantenal shall come. Blood-vomit shall come. Kukulcan shall come with them for the second time*[21]*."*
>
> *There will be scarcities of corn and squash during this katun that leads to a great loss of life. A plague will threaten beehives.*[22]

The most interesting part of this Mayan prediction for our present *katun* cycle that ends in 2012 is the first part: "It is the *katun* of remembering and recording knowledge." It was in our present cycle that the World Wide Web was invented!

The World Wide Web was created by Tim Berners-Lee and became publicly available on August 6, 1991 but really went under-utilized until 1993 with the creation of the

Mosaic web browser. According to Wikipedia, "Scholars generally agree that a turning point for the World Wide Web began with the introduction of the Mosaic web browser in 1993...."

Interestingly, Mosaic was released on April 22, 1993. As was stated earlier our present *katun*, *Katun 4 Ahau*, began on April 6, 1993. Interesting.

No technology has enabled the "remembering of knowledge and recording it" more so in the history of civilization than the World Wide Web. In just seconds one can access research on any topic in humanity's entire realm of knowledge. What used to require driving to a library, searching card catalogs, finding the book on the shelves and searching its index and table of contents to see if it had the information you were looking for can now be done in seconds from home. What is more, though, is no library could ever match the amount of information available via the Web thus the odds of finding what you are looking for is greatly increased on the Web than in a library.

More importantly, as Google CEO Eric Schmidt noted in 2010, every two days we create and record as much information as we did from the dawn of civilization up until 2003.[23] Just think about that for a second.

Thus, if you were a modern-day Mayan calendar priest, the arrival of the Web in the present *Katun 4 Ahau* period would not be very surprising and would seem to verify the perceived character and nature of the *Katun 4 Ahau* period.

The Mayan *katun* predictions are cyclic. *Katun 4 Ahau* repeated once every 256 years. So, let us back-test this theory and just as a Mayan Jaguar Priest would have done look back through recorded history at previous *Katun 4 Ahau* periods to see what events happened and if the pattern holds up.

The previous *Katun 4 Ahau* coincided with the years 1736-1756. Interestingly, the theoretical underpinnings of the Internet, known as graph theory, were first presented in 1735 and published in 1741. On August 26, 1735 Leonard Euler presented his solution to the mathematical problem known as the Seven Bridges of Konigsberg. The Internet utilizes a technique called packet switching to move data around the network that is only possible because of Euler's solution to the Seven Bridges mathematical problem. Thus it seems that discoveries in this *Katun 4 Ahau* cycle led directly to the fulfillment of a prediction in the **next** *Katun 4 Ahau* cycle.

According to Wikipedia it was also in 1728 and 1751 that the first modern encyclopedias were created. An encyclopedia certainly represents the idea of "remembering and recording knowledge."

The next prior *Katun 4 Ahau* cycle coincided with the years 1480-1500. This corresponds to the Age of Exploration as well as the invention of the printing press. According to Wikipedia, "by 1500, printing presses throughout western Europe had already produced more than 20 million volumes." It seems the printing press had the same impact on information during its time period that the World Wide Web did in its time period and both fell within a *Katun 4 Ahau* cycle. By 1620, Francis Bacon noted that printing had "changed the whole face and state of things throughout the world." The same quote could be used in regards to the World Wide Web today.

The next previous *Katun 4 Ahau* coincided with the years 1224-1244. Coincidentally, the most quoted Encyclopedia of the Middle Ages, the *De proprietatibus rerum*, was created in 1240 by Bartholomeus Anglicus.

The creation of encyclopedias, the printing press and the Web all during *Katun 4 Ahau* cycles does appear to support the Mayan belief that this katun cycle was associated with advances in the recording of information. Could their other beliefs about the nature of this cycle also be accurate? Let us now look at the other part of the Mayan predictions for *Katun 4 Ahau*, namely:

> *"Ah Kantenal shall come...There will be scarcities of corn and squash during this katun that leads to a great loss of life."*

According to one researcher, *Al Kantenal* means "he who adulterates maize."[24] Interestingly, it was in 1996 that the first genetically modified seeds came on the market. The first of these were corn, soybeans, and cotton. Genetically modified squash was introduced later. Fifteen years later around 86% of all corn grown in the U.S. is genetically modified thus there certainly is a "scarcity of corn," real corn, that is. The arrival of *Ah Kantenal*, "he who adulterates maize" would certainly seem to have been fulfilled as well.

As we have seen earlier, events that occur in one *katun* can apparently bring about the predictions the next time this *katun* cycle rolls around such as with the invention of graph theory in 1736 leading to the subsequent creation of the World Wide Web in 1993. Thus what is in store for the future?

One recent event in South Africa should give us all pause about the path we are currently on with genetically modified crops. In 2009 there was an **86% crop failure of genetically modified corn in South Africa**. Scientists still do not fully understand the cause. If the same were to happen in America, it would cause a worldwide food crisis.

Worse still is our agricultural industry currently plants only one variety of many of our most important food crops. This practice is called monoculture. The Maya, who first developed corn from wild grasses, always grew multiple varieties of corn. Plant diseases usually only affect one genetic variety; thus, if a disease breaks out that impacts one variety of corn it will not harm the other varieties. Famine is thus avoided by growing multiple varieties of a crop. Monoculture does not have this safeguard and disease can wipe out the entire crop. As Wikipedia notes:

> *There is currently a great deal of international worry about the wheat leaf rust fungus, that has already decimated wheat crops in Uganda and Kenya, and is starting to make inroads into Asia as well. As much of the worlds wheat crops are very genetically similar...the impacts of such diseases threaten agricultural production worldwide.*[25]

What will the state of the world's agricultural system look like 256 years from now when the next *Katun 4 Ahau* cycle rolls around? Global warming, peak oil, and genetically modified crop failures are all very real concerns for the future.

Additionally, between the years 1993 and 2012 there were several famines caused by the lack of corn. The southern African nations of Zimbabwe, Malawi, and Mozambique all experienced famines resulting from shortages of corn in the year 2002. North Korea experienced famines in 1996 and again in 2008. Thus "a great loss of life due to the scarcity of corn" seems to have happened just as the Mayan "prophecies" predicted.

Another Mayan prediction associated with agriculture was the one that stated, "*A plague will threaten beehives.*" It was in 2006 that a new disease causing the disappearance of countless beehives was first discovered and named Colony Collapse Disorder. According to Wikipedia, "Colony collapse is significant economically because many agricultural crops worldwide are pollinated by bees; and ecologically, because of the major role that bees play in the reproduction of plant communities in the wild."[26] Thus once again it seems a prediction for *Katun 4 Ahau* has come true.

What about the part of the "prophecy" or prediction that states, "Blood vomit shall come?" It is thought this references a disease experienced by the Maya during the *Katun 4 Ahau* cycle that immediately preceded the arrival of the Spanish in their lands. The sickness started with a fever followed by "body swelling and being filled with worms." The victim also vomited blood, hence the name. Some believe this disease was yellow fever.

Interestingly, in January of 1993 the first cases of Yellow Fever in Kenya were first diagnosed. They later determined that the outbreak had begun several months earlier. Kenya had never experienced a Yellow Fever outbreak in its entire history before this.

The "blood vomit" disease also sounds very similar to the effects caused by the Ebola virus. Several outbreaks of this virus have occurred since 1993 such as in 2000, 2001, 2004, and 2007. In fact, there have been more outbreaks of Ebola since 1993 than in all previous years. In this time period there were 18 known outbreaks that killed over 1,000 people. The mortality rate is staggering with the disease, which kills between 51%-83% of those who become infected. If this pathogen mutates so that it is more easily transmissible the world could have another Black Death on its hands. A global death toll between 51%-83% would not be the end of the world but would certainly be the end of the world as we know it.

There is one final part of the katun predictions for this cycle that is interesting. As the predictions state, "Kukulkan shall come." This refers to the arrival of the Toltec leader known as Topiltzen-Quetzalcoatl. (Kukulkan was the Mayan name for Quetzalcoatl.) This leader attempted to make reforms to violence-filled religious practices of the day that included child sacrifice. He commanded that instead of human sacrifices his followers should only sacrifice butterflies. This aroused the ire of the conservative religious authorities of the day whose power was threatened by this decree. Thus they persecuted him and drove him from their cities. He fled to the Yucatan peninsula where he took a leadership role at Chichen Itza.

In 2009 another leader took the world stage and on him the world pinned their hopes and dreams. That leader was Barack Obama. Articles written about him frequently used the terms "savior" and he was even given a Nobel Peace Prize within one year of being elected with the Nobel committee noting, "Only very rarely has a person to the same extent as Obama captured the world's attention and given its people hope for a better future."

More importantly, Obama was the first black President of the United States, undoubtedly one of the most powerful nations in the history of civilization. (Strangely enough, Obama has a sister named, of all things, Maya.)

A quick Google search reveals that, like Topiltzen-Quetzalcoatl, Obama was also attacked by conservatives and even accused of being an "anti-christ" and "socialist." He even issued an executive order, the first of his presidency, whereby the children of undocumented immigrants would no longer be "sacrificed", er, "deported." (Interestingly enough, most of these immigrants are descendants of the Maya and other Mesoamerican cultures.)

Obama's term happens to expire in 2012 and will be up for reelection just one month before the "end" of the Mayan calendar. Will he be expelled from Washington, DC just as Topiltzen-Quetzalcoatl was expelled from Tula?

Interestingly, all of the Founding Fathers of the United States were born in the previous *Katun 4 Ahau* cycle (1736-1756.) Thomas Jefferson was born in 1743. James Madison was born in 1751. Alexander Hamilton was born in 1755 and John Jay was born in 1745. All of these figures are today seen as "saviors" who were most responsible for the new Constitution. They also moved the capital from New York City (which Jefferson referred to as a "sewer of all depravities of human nature") and created a great new city, Washington, D.C., just as Topiltzen-Quetzalcoatl was forced to flee Tula and founded Chichen Itza whose great pyramid has become the *de facto* symbol for 2012.

These examples provide compelling evidence that the Mayan beliefs about the nature of the *katuns* and specifically the predictions for *Katun 4 Ahau* may have a sound basis. Perhaps the Maya over the course of centuries of careful observations discovered a cycle of predictable patterns that governs human civilization. As the Harvard economist and founder of the Foundation for the Study of Cycles, Edward Dewey, noted in 1967,

> *"Cycles are meaningful, and all science that has been developed in the absence of cycle knowledge is inadequate and partial. ...any theory of economics, sociology, history, medicine, or climatology that ignores non-chance rhythms is as manifestly incomplete as medicine was before the discovery of germs."*

It should also be remembered that **two** cycles come to an end on December 21, 2012. Not only does the smaller *Katun 4 Ahau* cycle end but also the 13th *baktun* of the larger 5,126-year "Great Cycle" which began on August 11, 3114 BC. Does this fact somehow amplify the events associated with the smaller *katun* cycle?

It seems that the creation of genetically modified

plants, the creation of the World Wide Web and the election of a black man to the position of leader of the most powerful nation on the planet are significant turning points in the history of civilization. Looking back over the past 5,126 years one will find nothing comparable. Thus it does seem that the two cycles ending together have somehow amplified the events of the smaller cycle.

In physics it is possible for two interacting waves or cycles to either cancel each other out or to add together and create an amplified wave. This is referred to as interference. Constructive interference is the name applied to the phenomenon of two waves (or cycles) creating an amplified wave/cycle. Thus it is quite possible that the underlying sources of energy behind these two Mayan cycles, solar and galactic, are interacting in such a way as to create an amplified cycle in the final years of the 13th *baktun* that coincides with *Katun 4 Ahau*.

There is one final "prophecy" or prediction for *Katun 4 Ahau* that we have yet to discuss which states, *"The quetzal shall come, the green bird shall come."* The quetzal refers to a bird known today as the Resplendent Quetzal. It has brilliant green and red feathers and excessively long green tail feathers. In fact, the term *quetzalli* was used by the Aztecs to refer specifically to these long green tail feathers which they used in their headdresses.

The Aztecs also combined the term *quetzal* with their word for snake, *coatl*, to name their deity Quetzalcoatl, also known as the Feathered Serpent or Plumed Serpent. Astronomers Napier & Clube in the groundbreaking book *The Cosmic Serpent* noted that stories surrounding this and other mythological sky serpents and dragons were likely representations of comets and meteors.

The choice of the *Quetzal* bird fits quite well with this theory with its long comet-like tail. The Chinese, in fact, referred to comets as "long-tailed pheasant stars" since they reminded them of the long tail feathers of pheasants. The choice of a bird combined with a snake helps to symbolically represent a snake-like entity located in the sky, which is a perfect description of a comet.

The color green seems to be another important part of this symbolism. *Quetzalcoatl* is usually represented as being green. In fact, the Aztec day sign "coatl" is a green rattle snake. Could this prophecy be a prediction of the appearance of a green comet between 1993-2012?

In fact, there have been three green comets between 1993-2012. The latest was in June 2010 when Comet McNaught became naked eye visible. The next previous was in February 2009 and was named Comet Lulin. Both of these were only barely visible to the naked eye for a few days thus they are not likely candidates to be included in such a momentous book of prophecy.

Yet four years prior on December 7, 2004 another green comet, Comet Machholz, became naked eye visible just a couple weeks before the Indonesian megaquake and tsunami. This event killed over 230,000 people in 14 countries making it one of the deadliest natural disasters in recorded history. This was the third largest earthquake ever recorded and produced a tsunami wave over 100 feet tall.

Comet Machholz was discovered on August 27, 2004. The comet's orbit was calculated to be about 12,500 years thus its last appearance was around 10,500 BC. At that time the Earth was in the midst of a global warming which was bringing an end to the last Ice Age. Yet something catastrophic occurred that plunged the Earth back into Ice Age conditions for another thousand years. The great megafauna of that age, including mastadons, mammoths, saber toothed tigers and more, all became extinct. Richard Firestone in his book *Cycles of Cosmic Catastrophes* theorized that a comet slammed into the Earth bringing about much of these changes.

Equally interesting as its green color is the fact that Comet Machholz passed near the Pleiades. The Pleiades were known as *"tzab,"* the rattlesnake rattles, to the ancient Maya. The rattlesnake uses its rattles as a warning before it strikes. Thus could the use of the green, long-tailed Quetzal bird combined with a rattlesnake in the *Quetzalcoatl* symbol have been created purposefully to encode the passing of a green comet near the Pleiades as a type of "early warning" system to warn future generations that this sequence of events signaled the beginning of a new age of disasters that happen once every 10,500 years?

Above: "Comet Machholz meets the Pleiades." © *Stefan Seip, Astromeeting.de*

In fact, since the discovery of Comet Machholz in August 2004, Earth has experienced some of its worst natural disasters in recorded history from the Indonesian and Japanese megaquakes and tsunamis to Hurricane Katrina. We are also in the midst of another global warming comparable in scale to that which ended the last Ice Age. We are also in the midst of one of the greatest extinction events since the last Ice Age. Are all of these things happening by chance or is there a natural cycle of cataclysms every 10,500 years that the orbit of Comet Machholz just happens to coincide with thus making a perfect early warning system? (This will be discussed more in-depth in chapter 7, "Comet Machholz and the Return of Kukulkan.")

The year 10,500 BC holds other significance as well. For instance, researcher Robert Bauval asserted in his book *The Orion Mystery* that "the relative positions of three main Ancient Egyptian pyramids on the Giza plateau are (by design) correlated with the relative positions of the three stars in the constellation of Orion which make up Orion's Belt— as these stars appeared 10,000 BC."[27] Researcher Graham Hancock asserted in his book *The Message of the Sphynx* that "the Great Sphinx was constructed c. 10,500 BC (Upper Paleolithic), and its lion-shape [was] maintained to be a definitive reference to the constellation of Leo."[28] Why were these monuments aligned to stars as they appeared 12,000 years ago and who built them?

In his book *Fingerprints of the Gods*, Hancock goes on to theorize that all of this could only be possible if a "previously enigmatic ancient but highly advanced civilization had existed in prehistory, one which served as the common progenitor civilization to all subsequent known ancient historical ones [and] sometime around the end of the last Ice Age this civilization ended in cataclysm, but passed on to its inheritors profound knowledge of such things as astronomy, architecture, and mathematics."[29] Did this same civilization pass on its myths about a green "sky serpent" whose return would signal the beginning of a new age of disasters?

Mainstream archaeologists and academics had for years dismissed the idea that any advanced ancient civilizations had existed that far back in time and that the earliest civilizations only arose around 3200 BC. Yet recent discoveries in Turkey of an ancient temple site called Göbekli Tepe that dates to 10,000 BC[30] has pushed back the accepted start of civilization another 7,000 years. Could the builders of this site be responsible for the transmission of this ancient myth about a green sky serpent to the Olmec, the mother culture of Mesoamerica who then passed it on to the Maya and Aztecs? (This proposition will be fully explored in chapter 21.) More importantly, what other discoveries lay hidden awaiting discovery in the future?

    This concludes my interpretation for a few of the prophecies for *Katun 4 Ahau*, the time period that ends on December 21, 2012. Yet this does not end the *katun* prophecies. In fact, the most dire prophecies were reserved for the years between 2032-2052. But first let us explore what the Maya predicted for the cycle named *Katun 2 Ahau* that begins on December 21, 2012 and continues for another twenty years until 2032. This will be the subject of the next chapter: "Predictions for *Katun 2 Ahau* (2012-2032)."

5. Predictions for Katun 2 Ahau (2012-2032)

As discussed in the previous chapter, "Predictions for *Katun 4 Ahau* (1993-2012)," the Maya made predictions in their prophetic books known as the *Chilam Balam* that seem to correspond with real events over the past 800 years. Yet these predictions do not end on December 21, 2012 thus clearly the Maya did not believe the world would end on this date. So what did the Maya believe would happen beyond 2012?

The Maya believed a new cycle known as *Katun 2 Ahau* began on December 21, 2012 and ended in 2032. According to Bruce Scofield in his book *Signs of Time: An Introduction to Mesoamerican Astrology*, the predictions for this twenty-year period were as follows:

> *For half of the katun there will be food, for half some misfortunes. This katun brings the end of "the word of God." It is a time of uniting for a cause.*

The Mayan *Katun* cycles repeated every 256 years thus, as in our previous article, it is instructive to do as a Mayan calendar priest would have done and look back at previous *Katun 2 Ahau* time periods and see what happened then to get a better idea of what to expect in the future.

The previous *Katun 2 Ahau* began in 1756 and ended in 1776. For Americans, this period represents the birth of ideas that led to their Revolution and the founding of their country. Thus it was certainly "a time of uniting for a cause."

Interestingly, this new country was founded on the principles of reason and not religious ideology. It was perhaps one of the first empires in history based on the idea that men could rule themselves without the need for god-kings. In fact, this new nation was the first in history to purposefully keep separate the religious sphere from the political sphere. Thus the founding of America did, indeed, see "the end of 'the word of God,'" in the political sphere. Laws were not based on the interpretation of ancient religious texts but instead on debate between reasonable men. A man-made Constitution interpreted by secular judges was the ultimate authority on the validity of a law and not the opinions of religious leaders (as is the case in Iran and other theocracies.) This truly represented a new model for humanity and these ideas would spread around the globe bringing profound changes over the next 250 years.

The next previous *Katun 2 Ahau* cycle corresponded to the years 1500-1520. This time period was the Age of Exploration and the first explorations of the New World. Again, this was certainly a "time of uniting for a cause." It was also a time that saw "the end of 'the word of God'" but this time it was the religions of the New World that came to an end. Religions throughout North and South America, which had been practiced for thousands of years, were replaced by Christianity and it all began in 1520 when the Aztec capital of Tenochtitlan in modern Mexico City was conquered.

Yet Christianity also underwent a major crisis during this time period as well. Martin Luther launched the Protestant Reformation in 1517. This revolution would eventually see the Catholic Church lose much of its power in world affairs. The Pope, in particular, once seen as God's sole representative on Earth, was completely cast out of the Protestant faith. The hierarchical structure of the priesthood and the view that priests were the sole mediators between the individual and God were both abandoned in favor of a direct relationship between the individual and God.

These were revolutionary ideas in the history of civilization and represented profound changes in religious practice. In fact, without the Protestant Reformation in the prior *Katun 2 Ahau* cycle could the American Revolution have happened at all? It seems the Protestant Reformation with its focus on the individual was the foundation upon which the American Revolution was built in the next *Katun 2 Ahau* cycle.

Thus the two prior occurrences of the *Katun 2 Ahau* cycle saw profound changes in the role of religion within society. What, then, can we expect for the next *Katun 2 Ahau* cycle that begins on December 21, 2012 and ends in 2032?

Already there have been very serious crises in the Catholic Church with the pedophile priest scandals. Will the next twenty years see the priesthood lose even more respect and power over their parishioners as a result? The American Catholic Church has already been separating itself from Rome over the past few decades. Will this separation grow stronger?

Islam has seen its own crisis recently with the rise of fundamentalist groups espousing a violent and repressive ideology. Will a "protestant reformation" happen within Islam that will lead to a loss of power for its religious leaders and a rise in the role of the individual and secular voices in the political sphere? Recent events in North Africa and the Middle East, the so-called Arab Spring, suggest such changes are already underway. If events of the last two *Katun 2 Ahau* cycles are any indication, these revolutions in the Muslim world should lead to long-term positive changes.

The first part of the Mayan predictions for *Katun 2 Ahau* is, by far, the most troubling: "for half the katun their will be food, for half misfortune." Previous occurrences of this cycle have, indeed, coincided with severe famines. Between 1756-1776 there was famine in Spain, Italy, India, Czech Republic, Germany and Sweden. Over ten million died in India alone. Between 1500-1520 there was famine in

Spain and Italy. Between 1244-1263 there was famine in Portugal, Germany and Italy.

Where will famine strike in the next *Katun 2 Ahau* cycle between 2012 and 2032? Worrying signs are already appearing in news headlines around the globe. Colony Collapse Disorder has seen the bee population reduced by as much as 30% which is significant since bees pollinate many of our food crops. There has also been a dramatic increase in the use of genetically modified food crops such as corn and soybeans. As noted in the previous chapter, an 80% crop failure was experienced with genetically modified corn in Africa with no known cause to date. If something similar happened to the American corn crop that consists primarily of genetically modified varieties, it would lead to a worldwide food crisis since much of the developing world relies on American surplus corn. It could also lead to drastic increases in the price of other staple foods leading to food riots similar to those seen before the recent financial crisis when commodity prices were soaring.

The continued environmental crisis could also lead to famines. Already important fish and mollusk species in the ocean have been collapsing due to overharvesting and pollution. Coral reefs, important breeding grounds for fish species, have been dying off at alarming rates due to acidification and warmer ocean temperatures. Climate change is also causing more severe droughts in once productive areas and causing more severe floods in others. Both of these situations can easily lead to severe famines in areas of the world that are not prepared to handle them through technologies such as irrigation and flood control. In fact, on September 3, 2012 CNN.com ran a story predicting a food crisis in 2013 due to droughts in the U.S., Australia, and Russia pushing global food costs up.[31]

Thus the cycle beginning on December 21, 2012 and ending in 2032 brings both positive and negative changes for civilization. The current trend of democratization of the world seems likely to continue as it spreads across the Muslim world. Yet the continued environmental crisis and use of genetically modified food crops could lead to severe famines during this time period as well.

6. Predictions for Katun 13 Ahau (2032-2052)

The Maya did not predict the end of the world on December 21, 2012. But they did predict major problems for civilization between the years 2032-2052. As noted in the two previous chapters on Mayan 2012 predictions, the Maya believed civilization operated on a 256-year cycle broken into thirteen 20-year periods known as the 'Cycle of 13 *Katuns*.' For each 20-year *katun* the Maya had a **prophecy or prediction** associated with it and as seen in the previous two chapters, these "prophecies" seem to contain accurate predictions for what actually happened during these time periods in the past.

The cycle that begins in 2032 and ends in 2052, named *Katun 13 Ahau*, is the last of the thirteen *katuns* in the current 256-year cycle that began in 1796. According to Bruce Scofield in his book *Signs of Time: An Introduction to Mesoamerican Astrology*, the prophecy recorded in the Mayan books known as the *Chilam Balam* for *Katun 13 Ahau* is as follows:

> *This is a time of total collapse where everything is lost. It is the time of the judgement of God. There will be epidemics and plagues and then famine. Governments will be lost to foreigners and wise men, and prophets will be lost.*

Since the Maya believed the *Katun* cycles repeated once every 256 years, it is helpful to look back at previous years associated with *Katun 13 Ahau* and see what happened then to be better able to foresee what might happen in the future.

The previous time period associated with *Katun 13 Ahau* was between 1776-1796. These were indeed momentous years for the world and the history of civilization because these years represented the birth of the

United States of America and modern democracy.

In 1776 the British colonies in America declared their independence from England. The most famous sentence from this declaration was the following:

We hold these truths to be self-evident, that all men are created equal, that they are endowed by their Creator with certain unalienable Rights, that among these are Life, Liberty and the pursuit of Happiness.

The impact of these words on human civilization cannot be underestimated. Not only did it lead to the American Revolution but these words would also form the foundation for the abolition of slavery and the equal rights of women and racial minorities.

Since the beginning of civilization, slavery and other forms of servitude and inequality had been a central, nearly unquestioned part of life. Kings and Pharaohs believed they not only derived their power from God but also were, in fact, descended genetically from God; thus, their power was not to be questioned by those they ruled over. They passed their power genetically down to their sons who inherited their father's throne and thus power stayed among a very small group of people.

This would all change with this one sentence from the Declaration of Independence. Over the next 256 years kings would be abolished or reduced to mere symbolic figureheads all over the world. Over this time period more and more classes of people would gain more and more rights. Thus the trend of the past 256 years starting in 1776 has been an increase in the rights of individuals. Thus for kings, it was definitely a time of total collapse where everything was lost. All the European empires would eventually collapse and the country whose Declaration of

Independence started the ball rolling would end up the one lone superpower in the world.

This reveals an important aspect of the Mayan predictions: they appear dependent upon one's point of view. From the point of view of kings, it was a time of total collapse. Since the ancient Egyptians 4,000 years prior, civilization had been based on kingship. The beginning of the end for this model of civilization arrived in 1776. But for the average person, it was not a time of total collapse but a time of ever-increasing rights and power.

The last year of the previous *Katun 13 Ahau* cycle was 1796. This was also a momentous year for humanity for it was then that the first President of the United States stepped down and refused to hold office beyond the two terms he had already served. For this act, King George III in England called Washington "the greatest man in the world" because it is a rare thing for a person in power to voluntarily give up that power.

George Washington never had opponents during his two elections and had he run again it is unlikely anyone would have challenged him and he would have easily served another term in office. Instead, he stepped down. Thus in 1796 the first *true* election was held in the world's youngest democracy. A peaceful transfer of power occurred which was a rare thing in world history.

The next previous *Katun 13 Ahau* cycle was between 1520-1539. This time period would see the fall of the major empires in North and South America: the Aztecs and Incas. Outbreaks of smallpox and other diseases would wipe out millions of native inhabitants. The Spanish explorations of the southeastern U.S. would wipe out tens of thousands of Native Americans through disease and warfare and bring about the collapse of many of the ancient Native American civilizations. Thus from the perspective of the native inhabitants of the New World, this cycle did, indeed, bring about all the negative events predicted in the *Chilam Balam* prophetic books.

Based on the preceding evidence, what can we expect between the years 2032-2052? One worrying bit of information comes from a U.S. Governmental Accountability Office (GAO) report in 2007 that noted by 2040 the world was expected to reach "peak oil."[32] According to Wikipedia, "peak oil is the point in time when the maximum rate of petroleum extraction is reached, after which the rate of production is expected to enter terminal decline."[33] According to the report currently there is no energy source that can replace oil for transportation purposes. Also the report stated, "While the consequences of peak oil would be felt globally, the United States, as the largest consumer of oil and one of the nations most heavily dependent on oil for transportation, may be particularly vulnerable."

As supplies of oil dwindle there will be increased competition to control the supplies that remain. This competition would likely take the form of warfare between the superpowers. Yet long before this the price of oil would continue going up causing the price of everything else from food to consumer goods to go up as well. In the past such price increases have led to great social unrest. Food riots have been the downfall of many regimes in the past.

Another worrying bit of information comes from the U.S. Congressional Budget Office. According to their current projections the CBO believes the budget of the United States is unsustainable at current levels and the **American economy will crash by 2037**. The global economy nearly crashed in 2008 due to a few financial and insurance institutions in the U.S. and elsewhere making bad business decisions thus illustrating the world financial system is more fragile than anyone knew. If the U.S. crashes in 2037 it would take the rest of the world with it. Combined with Peak Oil this could be a perfect storm of events that could bring the developed nations to their knees.

Yet a financial collapse and Peak Oil may not be the only threats we are faced with between 2032-2052. In 2004 NASA reported that the asteroid 99942 Apophis was on a collision course with Earth. It was originally calculated to impact Earth in 2029 but later calculations disproved that timeline. But these new calculations projected the asteroid might strike on Friday, April 13, 2036. Based on the size of the asteroid, NASA calculated that it would have an explosive impact of 510 megatons. By comparison, the Barringer Crater in Arizona was created 40,000 years ago by an impact of around 10 megatons.

Barringer Crater in Arizona. Apophis would be 50 times as powerful as the impact that created this crater. Courtesy NASA.

In November 2007 another asteroid named *2007 VK187* was also discovered to be on a collision course with Earth with a possible impact date on June 3, 2048. In January 2011 yet another asteroid named *2011 AG5* was found to be on a possible collision course with earth. Its expected impact date is February 5, 2040. Thus a total of three asteroids have a chance of slamming into earth during the 2032-2052 *katun* period. Worse still, what if the unthinkable happened and they all impacted earth during this time period?

The effects of an Apophis impact alone would be profound. According to astronomers Victor Clube and Bill Napier in the book *Cosmic Winter*, such an event would throw Earth into a global winter no matter where it struck and devastate thousands of square kilometers. But projected impact locations for 99942 Apophis include both the Pacific and Atlantic Oceans.

Astrophysicist Neil deGrasse Tyson has noted if the asteroid struck the Pacific it would create megatsunamis that would vaporize the entire west coast of North America.[34] If it struck the Atlantic Ocean, the mega tsunami would wipe out the entire east coast of the U.S. as well as the coastal areas in West Africa, South America, and Western Europe. The mega tsunami would travel miles inland destroying everything in its path then washing everything out to sea. Future archaeologists would find little to prove a civilization ever existed in these locations. As scientist Mike Baillie noted:

> *"If Apophis hits the earth the impact will be in the 3000-megaton class. It is entirely reasonable to state that such an impact, taking place anywhere on the planet, would collapse our current civilization and return the survivors, metaphorically speaking, to the Dark Ages (it is believed that in such an event globalised institutions, such as the financial and insurance markets would collapse, bringing down the entire interconnected monetary, trade and transport systems)."*[35]

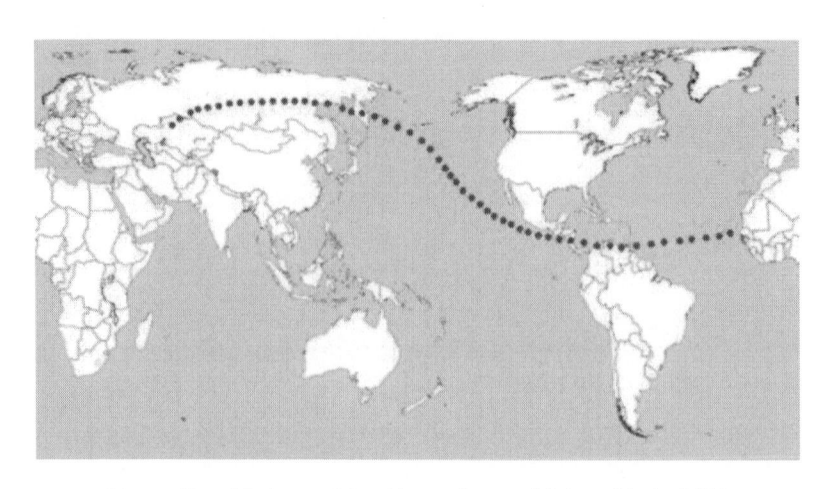

Above: Possible impact locations of asteroid Apophis in 2036

Combined with the financial collapse and Peak Oil, could the world much less America survive such a series of catastrophes? It would tax the world's resources in the best of times yet in the midst of a collapsing global financial system it seems improbable the world could pull itself back together. This could be a perfect storm of catastrophes that the developed world would be hard pressed to survive.

Yet the undeveloped world would actually fare better though not by much. Tribal communities around the globe who are already self-sufficient and not dependent on technology or global trade would feel little impact from the financial meltdown in the developed world. They would still herd their cattle and goats, grow their crops, gather their firewood and live their lives unaware that the world outside their small village had ceased to exist. The climate downturn would impact their ability to grow crops and may impact the food supply for their herds but they would still be able to hunt and gather.

Humans have survived such instances of cosmic catastrophe before. As Plato noted in his *Timaeus and Critias*:

> *"There have been, and will be again, many destructions of mankind arising out of many causes;*

the greatest have been brought about by the agencies of fire and water, and other lesser ones by innumerable other causes.

There is a story, which even you have preserved, that once upon a time Phaethon, the son of Helios, having yoked the steeds in his father's chariot, because he was not able to drive them in the path of his father, burnt up all that was upon the earth, and was himself destroyed by a thunderbolt. Now this has the form of a myth, but really signifies **a declination of the bodies moving in the heavens around the earth, and a great conflagration of things upon the earth, which recurs after long intervals;**...

Whereas just when you and other nations are beginning to be provided with letters and the other requisites of civilized life, after the usual interval, the stream from heaven, like a pestilence, comes pouring down, and leaves only those of you who are destitute of letters and education; and so you have to begin all over again like children, and know nothing of what happened in ancient times..."

It should be remembered that Plato wrote this over 2500 years ago around 300 BC. It should also be remembered that modern science didn't accept the fact that rocks fell from the sky until the 1800s. Furthermore, it was not until the 20th century that we discovered that these rocks could wipe out life on earth and that they impacted Earth at seemingly regular intervals. Thus how did Plato arrive at the same exact conclusions 2500 years before modern science? The only way is if his account was based on actual records from similar catastrophes in the past, which is exactly what he claimed. Plato stated his knowledge of these events came from records kept by priests in Egypt.

Just as the Plato story describes, western civilization has just acquired the requisites of civilized life and now possibly faces the stream from heaven that will pour down and end it all and only those "who are destitute of letters and education," i.e, those living in tribal villages unconnected with the modern world, will survive with only vague ideas about life outside their village. Thus only legends and myths will survive about our civilization and, as human nature seems to dictate, these legends and myths will be discounted as superstitious nonsense by the most educated of some future civilization until they, too, come face to face with a similar catastrophe.

Or perhaps the world will combine its resources and launch some means to deflect the asteroid from its current Earth-crossing orbit. And if successful, perhaps this near-death experience will have profound effects on civilization and help us to see how fragile civilization and life are…and how special too. Such awareness would certainly lead to greater cooperation among the nations, ushering in a whole new era in civilization. For a time at least.

III. Beyond 2012

7. Quest for the Truth about 2012 and Beyond

As mentioned in chapter 3, "Predictions for Katun 4 Ahau (1993-2012)," in August 2004 a new green comet was discovered and named Comet Machholz. Astronomers calculated the orbital period of comet Machholz as 12,500 years[36] meaning the last time it had visited Earth was in 10,500 BC. At that time geologists have noted Earth experienced a series of unimaginable catastrophes that included a great worldwide flood from glacial melt water, extensive continent-wide forest fires, a mass extinction that killed off the mammoths, mastodons and other Ice Age mega-fauna, the disappearance of North America's stone age inhabitants known as the Clovis Culture, and the end of a period of rapid global warming and the return of Ice Age conditions that would last a thousand years.

Coincidentally, since the return and discovery of Comet Machholz in August 2004 Earth has experienced some of the most severe storms and earthquakes in recorded history. Some of the most severe space weather including the most powerful solar flares and gamma ray bursts in recorded history also occurred since 2004. That year also had the most naked-eye visible comets ever recorded[37] which suggests an increase in the amount of space debris entering the solar system thereby increasing the odds of an impact with Earth. It was also in 2004 that NASA scientists discovered the asteroid Apophis was on a collision course with Earth.[38]

Climate scientists have predicted that due to global warming these severe weather events will only get worse in the future. Space weather scientists say the sun appears to have entered a new period of increased activity. Geologists have noted there has been an increase in major earthquakes along the Pacific Plate since 2004 and they also expect more of the same in the future.[39]

Is this all a coincidence or are these events part of a natural, predictable cycle that happens every 12,500 years and just so happens to correspond with the orbit of Comet Machholz? Were the ancient Maya aware of this cycle and did they encode it in their myths about the return of *Kukulkan*, a green sky serpent that devours humans, as a warning and a visible sign post in the heavens to alert when the next age of catastrophes would begin?

Does the calendar date of December 21, 2012, mark the end of our rather quiet and peaceful epoch and the beginning of a new age of disasters similar to those that befell Earth in 10,500 BC? Mayan predictions do not end in 2012. As noted in chapter 5, "Predictions for Katun 13 Ahau (2032-2052)," their most dire predictions for civilization were reserved for the years 2032-2052 which eerily correspond with NASA estimates that the asteroid Apophis has a chance of hitting Earth on Friday, April 13, 2037 and the asteroid 2011 AG5 could hit in 2040.

Finally, did other ancient civilizations such as the Greeks and Egyptians also encode this information into their myths and monuments to not only *warn* of the impending catastrophes but also show how to *survive* them? Is this the reason all the great pyramids on Earth seem to be constructed over tunnels and caves and all the ancient myths recall that the survivors of the last catastrophes emerged from caves and the underworld? Could this also be why Russia is currently building an underground city the size of Washington, DC under the Ural Mountains?[40]

These are the topics that we will explore. This section will be a search for the truth about 2012 that travels around the world and back through time to uncover the scientific truths behind some of mankind's most ancient myths.

Once again, like an ancient Mayan priest (or modern scientist), I will explore what happened in the past to better understand what may happen in the future. I will decode the ancient myths of the Maya and others to see what they may really be trying to tell us about events in our past and hence, about similar events in our future. My findings will be backed up with hard scientific data from fields including geology, archaeology, climate science, space science, genetics, and more.

These chapters are not meant to be the definitive interpretation of these ancient myths. They are simply meant to open the reader's mind to the possibilities that these myths are not "mythical" and perhaps encode real information about the past. Much of the *strangeness* of these myths simply evaporates when one can compare their details with actual events. It is at that point that they stop sounding like superstitious nonsense and start to sound like accurate eyewitness accounts of real events.

Far from being an act of "doom and gloom" scare-mongering, decoding these myths actually provides "awareness and hope." Awareness of the fact that unimaginable catastrophes have happened in our past that could happen again in our future and hope because these myths reveal that not only are these catastrophes survivable but they give clues about *how* people survived.

The fact is each and every one of us is descended from ancestors who survived all of these unimaginable catastrophes throughout earth's history. The DNA inside of you right now came from your ancestors who survived droughts, plagues, famines, wars, floods, impact events and more. You are already one of the lucky ones, one of the survivors. Whatever the future has in store can be no worse than what your ancestors have already lived through and survived. Thus keep that in mind as you read the next few chapters.

8. Comet Machholz and the Return of Kukulkan

As stated in their prophetic book *Chilam Balam of Chumayel*, the Maya predicted that between April 6, 1993, and December 21, 2012, (a period they named *Katun 4 Ahau*):

> *"The quetzal shall come, the green bird shall come...Kukulcan shall come with them for the second time..."*

Kukulcan was the Mayan name for the Aztec deity *Quetzalcoatl*. Both Kukulcan and Quetzalcoatl meant "feathered serpent" in their respective languages. Astronomers William Napier and Victor Clube argued in their books *The Cosmic Serpent* and *The Cosmic Winter* that sky serpents, dragons and other such mythological beings were metaphors ancient astronomers used for comets. Is there any evidence that might support such an astronomical interpretation for Quetzalcoatl?

Above: Quetzalcoatl, the feathered serpent, shown devouring a human victim. (See color version on back cover.)

Quetzalcoatl was associated with Venus, the brightest 'star' in the night sky, thus we know the Maya and Aztecs believed Quetzalcoatl was a 'star.' (Of course we know Venus is a planet, not a star, thus it is more accurate to say they believed Quetzalcoatl was a bright light in the sky.) Strangely, early Spanish chroniclers noted that these Mexican cultures referred to Venus as "la estrella que humeava" or "the star that smoked."[41] Likewise, they referred to a comet as "a star that smoked." Therefore we see Venus and thus Quetzalcoatl were, indeed, associated with comets.

The other descriptions of Quetzalcoatl were that he arrived from the east, was bearded and wore a long robe, eventually departed and promised to return in the future. Does any of this symbolism also relate to comets?

In Europe comets were often referred to as "bearded stars" and modern astronomers also use the term "bearded" in reference to comets:

> "...when the comet is east of the sun, and moves from him, it is said to be bearded, because the light precedes it in the manner of a beard..."[42]

It was also common to describe comets and their long tails as stars wearing long robes. For instance, on a print by Friedrick Madeweis from 1681 that documented the path of Kirch's Comet across the sky it included a reference to the "long trailing robe"[43] of its tail.

Above: Friedrich Madeweis illustration of Comet Kirch with text noting its "long trailing robe."

Could the image of beards and robes combined as an old bearded man wearing a long robe be a way ancient astronomers represented comets? This seems to be the case for Quetzalcoatl. Likewise, the other elements of this myth, i.e., rising in the east, departing and returning in the future are all consistent with the interpretation of Quetzalcoatl as a comet.

Quetzalcoatl is composed of two words: *quetzal* + *coatl*. *Quetzal* refers to feathers and *coatl* refers to a snake thus the traditional translation of Quetzalcoatl is "feathered serpent."

Yet *quetzal* does not simply refer to any old feathers of any old bird. Quetzal refers specifically to the bright green tail feathers of the Resplendent Quetzal bird from southern Mexico. Of all the birds the Maya and Aztecs could have used to represent Quetzalcoatl, they chose the Resplendent Quetzal. Why?

The Resplendent Quetzal, known simply as the

Quetzal to Mexican peoples, is known for its brilliant green feathers. More specifically, the Quetzal is known for its long green tail feathers. The tail feathers of the Quetzal are longer than the entire body length of the bird. A bird that flies across the sky with a really long tail is a logical choice if the Maya intended to represent a comet.

Above: Resplendant Quetzal from southern Mexico ©Kenneth Lilly/Dorling Kindersley RF/Getty Images (See color version on back cover.)

The Chinese also likened a comet's tail to that of a bird's tail feathers. The Chinese referred to comets as "long-tailed pheasant stars"[44] since pheasants had very long tail feathers. Thus it is not completely unheard of for a culture to associate a bird's long tail feathers with the tail of a comet.

Comets can also *look* like a feather. On June 2, 1858 Donati's Comet was discovered by Italian astronomer

Giovanni Donati.[45] Drawings and paintings of this comet all reveal a comet whose tail had a feather-like appearance.

Above: Illustration of feather-like appearance of Donati's Comet over Paris in 1858.

    Was the color green another important reason the Mesoamerican cultures chose the Quetzal bird or was it chosen primarily for its long comet-like tail feathers and the color was incidental? Most of the images of Quetzalcoatl portray the deity as a green serpent. Even the Aztec calendar day sign *coatl* was depicted as a green snake in their religious picture book, the *Codex Magliabechiano*[46]. Thus the color green appears to have been an important aspect of Quetzalcoatl.

Above: Coatl glyph from Codex Magliabechiano. (See color version on back cover.)

What were the associations for the second part of the name: *coatl*? In the Aztec language *coatl* meant snake or serpent. Snakes appear to only have a head and a long tail just like a comet. Interestingly, in the Mayan language the word for snake and sky are the same. Thus Kukulkan, the Mayan name for Quetzalcoatl, has the following associations: feathered, sky, serpent.

Yet, just as *quetzal* did not represent any old bird, *coatl* did not represent just any old snake. Specifically, it represented the rattlesnake. Why would Mesoamerican cultures choose a rattlesnake to symbolize a green comet?

The Maya had one asterism, or star group, which was associated with the rattles of a rattlesnake: the Pleiades[47]. *Tzab-ek*, the Mayan name for this asterism, meant "rattlesnake rattles star." Rattlesnakes were often depicted throughout Mexico with four rattles, which likely corresponded to the four brightest stars of the Pleiades. The *kan* suffix in Kukulkan not only meant "serpent" and "sky" but also "four" which further supports this idea. This symbolism suggests the green comet is therefore associated with the Pleiades.

In the period of *Katun 4 Ahau* (1993-2012) were there any green comets associated with the Pleiades? Since 1993 there have been three green comets but only one was associated with the Pleiades: Comet Machholz. Comet Machholz was first discovered in August 2004 and became naked eye visible in November of that year. It reached its brightest level on January 7, 2005. At this time it also made its closest approach to the Pleiades. In fact, the tail of the comet entered the Pleiades[48] thus giving this green sky serpent its rattles! The return of Kukulkan, the green cosmic rattlesnake, appears to have occurred just as the Mayan 'prophecies' predicted.*

---

* As stated several times, the *katun* prophecies repeated every 256 years thus wouldn't this mean the Maya believed this comet would have returned every 256 years thereby invalidating the previous conclusion of a 12,500 year cycle? Astronomer and Mayan scholar Maud Makemson argued in her book *The Book of the Jaguar Priest* that many of the *katun* prophecies were likely earlier related to the *baktuns* and when the Maya stopped using the Long Count calendar the priests simply converted these *baktun* prophecies into *katun* prophecies. Yet this does not completely solve the problem for if this was true then it suggests the Maya believed this comet returned once every 5000 years. Thus could the Kukulkan prophecy have been unrelated to neither the *katun* or *baktun* cycles? The key words in this particular prophecy that support this possibility are, "Kukulcan shall come with them for the *second* time." If this event were supposed to have happened once every 256 years then why would the Maya specify that this return was the *second* one? Perhaps this phrase was to alert a future Mayan calendar priest that this particular prophecy would only be fulfilled in the *Katun 4 Ahau* period at the end of the Long Count 'Great Cycle' in 2012.

Above: "Comet Machholz meets the Pleiades" © Stefan Seip, Astromeeting.de
(See color version on back cover.)

9. Prelude to Disaster?

Yet, as noted previously, Comet Machholz is a long period comet with an orbital period of 12,500 years.[49] This means the last time anyone on Earth would have seen this comet (and thus been able to calculate its return) was in the year 10,500 BC. Could the Maya have had access to astronomical data going back that far in history?

Scholars have noted that the Mayan concept of the four world directions being associated with four different colors is remarkably similar to cultural practices in Asia and thus likely has origins in deep antiquity[50]; i.e., it came with them when their ancestors migrated across the Bering land bridge from Siberia at the close of the last Ice Age. Thus, at least one aspect of Mayan cultural practices still practiced today dates to that time period; thus, why not astronomical information encoded in their mythology?

More importantly, what message were the ancient Maya trying to convey by encoding the year 10,500 BC into their prophetic books? Since it is known that the Maya believed time was cyclical and that past events would reoccur in the future, did something happen in 10,500 BC which they felt might repeat again in the future?

In fact, one of the worst catastrophes ever to affect life on Earth occurred around 10,500 BC. Before this date, Earth had experienced rapid global warming which resulted in the melting of the glaciers from the last Ice Age raising sea levels hundreds of feet. Yet in 10,500 BC a catastrophe seems to have struck Earth. Temperatures plummeted as Earth entered a new period of extreme cold known as the Younger Dryas climate event.[51] In fact, this abrupt climate change happened within the course of only a few months![52]

This was brought about by the collapse of an ice dam that allowed the enormous glacier lake known as Lake

Agassiz to catastrophically dump its contents into the Arctic Ocean and North Atlantic. This influx of cold water shut down currents in the Atlantic which brought warm water up from the tropics to the northern hemisphere. Without this warm water the northern hemisphere reentered the Ice Age for another thousand years.

It was also at this time that mastodons, mammoths, and other mega-fauna all became extinct and the people known as the Clovis Culture disappeared from North America. Scientists consider this the most severe mass extinction since the dinosaurs disappeared 65 million years ago. Ninety-five percent of all large mammals went extinct but small animals were affected too. For example, ten genera of birds went extinct at this time. Such an event would clearly have left a strong cultural memory in the myths and legends of the survivors.

Although this event affected North America the most, it also severely impacted Europe, Siberia, and South America. In their book *The Cycle of Cosmic Catastrophes: How a Stone-Age Comet Changed the Course of World Culture*, scientists Richard Firestone and Allen West argued that the impact of a comet or meteor caused both the mass extinction and climate event.

In order to validate a theory one must be able to make predictions and then verify those predictions with research data. Therefore, if comet Machholz was the basis of the Kukulkan myth then it would follow that Kukulkan should be associated with disasters, especially flooding, such as what happened at the onset of the Younger Dryas when comet Machholz last appeared. Is there any evidence that the Maya and other Mesoamerican cultures associated Kukulkan/Quetzalcoatl with floods and disasters?

There is, in actuality, an abundance of evidence that the "sky serpent" was associated with floods and disasters.

The earliest site in Mesoamerica dedicated to the worship of Quetzalcoatl was at Teotihuacan. A mural at Teotihuacan showed a flood of water streaming from the mouth of a great green serpent. A great flood caused by a "sky serpent" also occurred in the Mayan books known as the *Dresden Codex*, the *Madrid Codex* and the *Popol Vuh*.

Above: Teotihuacan mural shows a flood being emitted from the mouth of a green feathered serpent. (See color version on back cover.)

In the *Popol Vuh* the deity known as *Hunab Ku*, "Heart of Heaven" (aka *Kukulkan*, *Hurakan*) destroyed the world by flood. Likewise, the *Dresden Codex* showed an image of the same giant serpent as seen at Teotihuacan with a torrent of water coming from its mouth. In this case, the story was also associated with Mayan deities known as the four *Bacabs* who were responsible for holding up the sky. According to this myth they did not do their job and the sky fell. The *Bacabs* were associated with the Pleiades and likely represented the four brightest stars of this asterism. (Coincidentally, the ancient Greek deity Atlas was associated with holding up the sky and was also associated with the Pleiades since the seven stars were seen as his seven daughters. One of these daughters was named, interestingly enough, Maia and another, Electra, was transformed into a comet.)

Above: Page from the Dresden Codex showing a flood of water coming from the mouth of a green serpent. Also shows the goddess Ixchel with a green snake on her head pouring water from a jar. (See color version on back cover.)

In the *Madrid Codex* a similar story of a deluge is illustrated by a serpent that tore a hole in the sky.[53] In this case the serpent was blue yet in the Mayan language the same word, *yax*, is used for both blue and green, which shows they made no distinction between these two colors. Thus a blue serpent could easily serve in place of a green one.

Above: This scene from the Madrid Codex shows a blue serpent tearing a hole in the sky which led to a flood. (See color version on back cover.)

It seems clear, then, that the Maya associated a green sky serpent with a catastrophic flood. According to their legends, this flood also brought about the end of a race of human beings.

Scientists also believe that the catastrophic events at the onset of the Younger Dryas were caused by a comet or comet fragments that impacted the Earth.[54] Archaeological evidence suggests a group of hunter-gatherers known as the Clovis Culture disappeared from North America at this time as well. Due to the similarity between Clovis stone tools and those of the Solutreans in France, some have even argued that the Clovis Culture were Europeans.[55] Thus the scientific evidence of a catastrophe associated with a comet that included a flood and the disappearance of a race of people matches Mayan mythology quite closely.

Yet scientists think fragments from comet Encke, not Machholz, impacted Earth and brought about these catastrophes.[56] In fact, every year we pass through the debris field from this comet. This debris causes the Taurid meteor showers each Fall around Halloween. These meteors appear to emanate from the Pleiades asterism in the constellation Taurus. Perhaps comet Machholz and thus *Kukulkan* were not the *cause* of the catastrophe but arrived before it and were later interpreted as a herald or messenger of the catastrophic floods that followed?

Interestingly, *Quetzalcoatl/Kukulkan* was also associated with the invention of writing and the arts; thus, he was a god of communication, a messenger god. According to one interpretation, "His mission was to establish communication between Heaven and Earth...."[57] What was the message Quetzalcoatl was to deliver?

Images of Quetzalcoatl showed a green-feathered serpent devouring a man. This suggests Quetzalcoatl was associated with death and destruction. Thus Quetzalcoatl was like a herald whose appearance foretold of devastations to follow. Comets were often used for this purpose across all cultures throughout history, which further supports the idea Quetzalcoatl was meant to represent a comet.

Quetzalcoatl's association with death and destruction was the rationale behind the Mesoamerican practice of human sacrifice. They believed these 'deities' were behind the natural disasters that consumed tens of thousands of lives. They believed they could appease this blood-thirst and avoid these catastrophes by sacrificing people to these 'gods.' Of course the people they chose for sacrifice were their enemies. If the gods needed blood, they reasoned, then the blood of their enemies should suffice thereby saving their own people from future catastrophes. There was a logical, if not perverse, calculus and method to the madness of human sacrifice.

Is this why the Maya chose a rattlesnake as opposed to some less deadly serpent to represent Quetzalcoatl? It should be remembered that a rattlesnake shakes its rattles as a warning before it strikes and unleashes its deadly venom. Did the Maya associate the Pleiades with rattlesnake rattles also as a way to encode the idea that these stars could serve as an early warning system before a catastrophe or series of catastrophes?

In addition to "serpent", *coatl* also had a second meaning: "twin." In Aztec mythology *Quetzalcoatl* had a twin known as *Xolotl*. *Xolotl* was associated with sickness, deformity, misfortune, and dogs (a taboo animal to the Aztecs).[58] His job was to guide souls to the underworld. (In one myth Quetzalcoatl also visited the underworld after a great flood and used his own blood to recreate humans to repopulate the Earth.[59])

It seems the mythological figure Quetzalcoatl perfectly encodes the idea of a green comet that passes near the Pleiades. Since the events of 10,500 BC had global impacts it should follow that other cultures around the world would also have encoded them in their myths. Can we find any other ancient myths that shared traits of Quetzalcoatl that will help support this idea? Indeed, another mythological figure is also associated with twin-winged serpents, the Pleiades, the underworld and a green comet: Hermes.

10. Quetzalcoatl & Hermes: Cosmic Messengers?

The symbol for Hermes in Greek mythology is the Caduceus or Staff of Hermes. This symbol consists of two serpents intertwined around a pole surmounted by a pair of wings. Thus the idea of twin serpents and wings were associated with both Hermes and Quetzalcoatl.

Like Quetzalcoatl, Hermes also was associated with the invention of writing and the arts and considered a messenger god. Hermes may be derived from Hermeneus, which means the interpreter.[60] From Hermes comes our word "hermeneutics," the study and theory of interpretation. He was also a god of commerce and of thieves. Like Quetzalcoatl and his twin Xolotl, Hermes guided souls to the underworld.

Hermes had several stellar associations. In Greek mythology he was the child of Zeus and Maia (pronounced identically to Maya). Maia was one of the stars of the Pleiades and was herself the daughter of Atlas. Atlas, like the Mayan Bacabs, was responsible for holding up the heavens. According to researcher Jacqueline Brook, Hermes was also associated with a green comet.[61]

To the Romans, Hermes was known as Mercury. According to legend, the green comet of Mercury was associated with "lightning's, thunders, earthquakes, great winds, violent storms, and new arts, always destructive for mankind."[62]

Quetzalcoatl had a wind aspect known as Ehecatl-Quetzalcoatl whose symbol was a swirling wind design. To the Maya this aspect of Quetzalcoatl was known as Hurakan where the modern word hurricane originates. Thus we see both Quetzalcoatl and Mercury/Hermes were associated with great winds, violent storms, and a green comet.

How well does all the preceding evidence correlate with Comet Machholz? In August 2004 comet Machholz was first discovered. This coincided with the start of the Atlantic hurricane season, which climate scientists had predicted would be uneventful. Yet the 2004 hurricane season was "one of the deadliest and most costly Atlantic hurricane seasons on record" with "one of the highest Accumulated Cyclone Energy totals ever observed."[63]

In fact, there were eight named storms that formed during August despite a weak El Nino that emerged that summer. "In an average summer, only three or four storms would be named in August. The formation of eight named storms in August [broke] the old record...."[64] The highest number of tornadoes ever recorded also occurred in 2004.

On Christmas day in December 2004 the third largest

earthquake ever recorded occurred off the west coast of Sumatra, Indonesia. The earthquake spawned tsunamis that killed over 230,000 people in fourteen countries making this event one of the deadliest natural disasters in recorded history.[65]

This rare event coincided with the brightest gamma ray burst ever recorded. This gamma ray burst came from a star only 12 miles across on the other side of our galaxy and released more energy in a tenth of a second than the sun emits in 100,000 years.[66]

The burst also affected Earth's ionosphere, briefly expanding it similarly to what happens during solar flares. The fact that a star so far away could affect Earth's ionosphere was a great surprise to the scientists who discovered it.

Physicist Dr. Paul LaViolette has theorized that such gamma ray bursts are preceded by gravity waves that can cause earthquakes on Earth.[67] Dr. LaViolette calculated that such a gravity wave would have arrived around the same time as the 2004 Indonesian megaquake that caused the tsunami. Dr. LaViolette calculated that the odds were extremely small that two such rare and powerful events could occur together and be unrelated.

On December 7, 2004 Comet Machholz became naked-eye visible just weeks before the megaquake and gamma ray burst. Then on January 7, 2005, Comet Machholz made its closest visit to the Pleiades. Just thirteen days later a solar flare "released the highest concentration of protons ever directly measured, taking only 15 minutes after observation to reach Earth...."[68]

Protons can cause severe damage to body tissues leading to radiation sickness and death. Typically the protons from such flares take an hour or more to reach Earth giving astronauts plenty of time to take shelter. Yet this time they travelled nearly the speed of light.[69]

It also should be noted that the strongest solar flare ever measured occurred on November 4, 2003, just nine months before the discovery of Comet Machholz. Other large solar flares have taken place on October 28, 2003, September 7, 2005, and February 17, 2011. In fact, "from January 2005 to September 2005 [Earth] experienced 4 severe geomagnetic storms and 14 X [class] flares."[70]

Could the green comet of Hermes/Quetzalcoatl be associated not only with increased terrestrial storms but also increased solar storms? Mercury, the Roman version of Hermes, is always shown wearing a solar hat thus clearly has solar associations.

Likewise, the type of snake associated with Quetzalcoatl was the rattlesnake species *Crotalus durissus*. Researchers have noted that this rattlesnake has a design near its rattles that is identical to the Mayan glyph *ahau* that "designates the Sun God."[71] Thus in addition to encoding the concepts of "twin" and "serpent," *coatl* also encoded the concept of "sun." There were other species of rattlesnake they could have used to symbolize Quetzalcoatl but they chose the *Crotalus durissus* with the *ahau* symbol on its tail. In light of all the evidence this seems quite purposeful.

Usually humanity is protected from solar storms by Earth's magnetic field but in 2008 NASA scientists discovered a huge hole in this field "ten times larger than anything previously thought to exist….The entire day-side of the magnetosphere was open to the solar wind."[72]

Any major flares occurring at that time would have hit Earth unimpeded by the protective magnetic field and caused immense damage to both life and technological infrastructure.

Has the sun entered a new phase of activity that could pose dangers to Earth in the near future? Is this why the Maya referred to the beginning of a new age as the birth of a new sun? Is it the sun causing an increase in storm activity? Is the sun, in fact, the root cause of global warming and not carbon dioxide?

Astronomer Sallie Baliunas and astrophysicist Willie Soon, researchers at Harvard-Smithsonian Center for Astrophysics, have shown that "changes in the Sun can account for major climate changes on Earth for the past 300 years, including part of the recent surge of global warming...[and] heat-trapping gases emitted by smokestacks and vehicles -- the so-called greenhouse effect -- appear to be secondary."[73]

A few months after the January 2005 solar flare, the Atlantic hurricane season began. This was "the most active Atlantic hurricane season in recorded history [with] a record twenty-eight tropical and subtropical storms formed, of which a record 15 became hurricanes. Of these, seven strengthened into major hurricanes, a record-tying five became Category 4 hurricanes and a record four reached Category 5 strength.... Among these Category 5 storms were Hurricanes Katrina and Wilma, respectively the costliest and the most intense Atlantic hurricanes on record."[74]

Since 2005 some of the largest and/or deadliest natural disasters in recorded history have occurred including the 2005 Kasmir earthquake (79,000 dead), 2006 Java earthquake, 2008 Sichuan earthquake (61,000 dead), 2008 Cyclone Nargis (138,000 dead), 2010 Chile earthquake and tsunami (8.8 magnitude), 2010 Haiti earthquake and tsunami (222,000 dead), & the 2011 Tohoku Japan earthquake and tsunami (20,000 dead). [75]

This period also included two of the deadliest avalanches in history (2010 Salang & Kohistan avalanches in

Afghanistan and Pakistan respectively) and two of the deadliest blizzards (2008 Afghanistan blizzard & 2008 Chinese winter storms). It also included two of the deadliest heat waves in history: Europe 2003 (40,000 dead) & Russia 2010 (56,000 dead) and two of the deadliest non-cyclone storms both in Brazil, 2008 (128 dead) and 2011 (1,000 dead).[76]

The most tornadoes to touch down in a single day, 312, occurred on April 28, 2011, which was double the previous record.[77] In May 2011 flooding on the Mississippi River broke records in many locations.

We have seen that since Comet Machholz arrived Earth has entered a period of extreme natural disasters. Two of the top ten deadliest natural disasters of all time have happened since 2004: the 2004 Indian Ocean Tsunami and the 2010 earthquake in Haiti. Thus the green comet of Mercury-Hermes-Quetzalcoatl being associated with "lightning's, thunders, earthquakes, great winds, [and] violent storms" seems fitting and just a little more than coincidental.

Hermes was also a god of commerce and of thieves. Coincidentally, in 2008 the worst financial crisis in history struck the entire world.

There is no known mechanism for a comet to be the source of such disasters nor do the ancient myths suggest this. The myths about Quetzalcoatl and Hermes suggest that a green comet serves as a herald or messenger of extreme catastrophes to come. If this is the case, then it would appear that there is a natural cycle of catastrophes with which the orbit of Comet Machholz just happens to coincide. Thus the next obvious questions are what is the orbit of Comet Machholz and when was the last time it visited Earth and what were the consequences?

11. Younger Dryas Climate Event & the Clovis Comet

According to astronomers, Comet Machholz is a long period comet with a 12,500-year orbital period. The last time Comet Machholz visited Earth was in 10,500 BC. This corresponded to the beginning of the Younger Dryas climate event that saw parts of the world become much cooler. Earth had experienced a global warming that was bringing an end to the Ice Age. Yet something happened in 10,500BC that reversed this global warming trend. A great mass extinction also occurred at this time with the die off of the mega-fauna such as mammoths, mastodons, giant sloths, saber toothed tigers and more. The Clovis Culture in North America also ended.[78]

What caused this climate event? It appears that an enormous fresh water lake known as Lake Agassiz existed in the center of North America created from the melt water of the glaciers covering the continent then. This lake covered over 440,000 square miles and was larger than all the Great Lakes combined and held more water than all of today's lakes combined! Around 10,500 BC an ice dam collapsed and the lake catastrophically drained north into the Arctic Ocean.[79]

This influx of cold water shut down the currents in the Atlantic Ocean that transferred the warm equatorial waters north. This led to a return of Ice Age conditions for much of the northern hemisphere. It also led to immense coastal flooding as sea levels rose hundreds of feet as a result of the melting.

What caused the ice dam to melt? One theory suggests a comet exploded over the ice sheet. Richard Firestone of the U.S. Department of Energy's Lawrence Berkeley Laboratory noted, "Our research indicates that a 10-kilometer-wide comet, which may have been composed from the remnants of a supernova explosion, could have hit North America 13,000 years ago. This event was preceded by an intense blast of iron-rich grains that impacted the planet roughly 34,000 years ago."[80]

According to this theory a swarm of comets impacted Earth and/or exploded in the atmosphere with the same destructive power as a nuclear war. This caused immense fire storms that set much of the world's forests ablaze. Evidence of this global conflagration can be seen in the geologic record as a 'black mat' that appears just before the layer representing the onset of the Younger Dryas climate event. This 'black mat' layer has been found in North America, South America and Europe suggesting a worldwide catastrophe.

Meteorites with a lunar origin have also been found on Earth that also date to this time which suggests that the moon was also impacted by comets which resulted in lunar rocks being ejected into space and then falling to Earth. In fact, the Toba tribe in South America claimed a world fire was caused when pieces of the moon broke and struck Earth.[81]

Yet could these forest fires have had an additional cause? Could the sun have erupted with a super solar flare that was intense enough to set forests ablaze?

12. Super Solar Flares

Scientists studying Greenland ice cores have noted that the Younger Dryas period is bracketed by two nitrate spikes in the ice record.[82] Scientists have noted that nitrate spikes in more modern ice core samples dating back to 1561 coincide with known solar flare events. The largest such nitrate spike coincides with the 1859 Carrington Event which was the first solar flare ever observed by modern astronomers. It was the result of a Solar Superstorm and it produced auroras as far south as the Caribbean.[83]

The telegraph was the only form of technology that existed in 1859. According to Wikipedia, "Telegraph systems all over Europe and North America failed in some cases even shocking telegraph operators. Telegraph pylons threw sparks and telegraph paper spontaneously caught fire. Some telegraph systems appeared to continue to send and receive messages despite having been disconnected from their power supplies."[84] A study conducted by the National Science Foundation to determine what would happen if a Carrington size solar storm were to occur today concluded the U.S. would be without power for years as a result.

The nitrate spikes bracketing the Younger Dryas period are substantially higher than those produced by the Carrington Event. This suggests the solar storm that produced them was orders of magnitude larger. Could such a storm be powerful enough to set forests on fire?

The answer came when the Apollo 11 astronauts landed on the moon. They discovered small lunar craters that showed signs of glazing on their exposed surfaces. In 1969 astrophysicist Thomas Gold concluded that "radiation intensity on the Moon had reached 100 suns for 10 to 100 seconds…"[85] to produce such glazing.

Humans appear to not only have witnessed such an event but also to have recorded it on petroglyphs around the world. Physicist Anythony Peratt of the Los Alamos National Laboratory noted that literally thousands of petroglyphs around the world showed abstract designs that were identical to patterns made by high-energy plasma discharges in the laboratory.[86]

How could ancient people over 12,000 years ago have created such designs? The only way, theorizes Peratt, is if the sun unleashed a high-energy solar flare orders of magnitude larger than any in recorded history that produced these plasma designs as auroras in the sky. The ancient sky watchers then simply carved into the rock the designs they were seeing in the sky.

One design that appeared in many places around the world was a stick figure man sometimes with a birdlike head. Dr. Peratt was able to reproduce this design with plasma discharges in the laboratory.

13. Thoth, the Egyptian Messenger of the Sun God

Interestingly, the ancient Egyptians had a deity known as Thoth who was represented as a bird-headed man. Thoth shared all the qualities and characteristics of both Quetzalcoatl and Hermes. When the ancient Greeks ruled over Egypt they also noted the similarities between Hermes and Thoth and considered them to be the same god.

Above: Thoth (Courtesy Wikipedia)

Like Hermes and Quetzalcoatl, Thoth was a god of communication and the inventor of hieroglyphic writing as well as responsible for guiding souls to the underworld. He was also depicted as a "dog faced baboon[87]," similar to depictions of Quetzalcoatl's twin Xolotl.

He was also considered the heart of the sun god Ra. Interestingly, Quetzalcoatl's wind aspect called Ehecatl-

Quetzalcoatl or Hurakan was also known as "heart of sky." In Mayan myth Hurakan is said to have caused the Great Flood.[88] Thoth was also considered not only the heart (or mind) of Ra but also the tongue as well which symbolized he was the means by which Ra's will was translated into speech[89], i.e., he was a messenger of the Sun.

Interestingly, the hieroglyphs used to write his name included a twin-serpents glyph similar to the caduceus or staff of Hermes and a bird glyph. Thus just like Quetzalcoatl and Hermes he was associated with both twin serpents and wings. Since Thoth (like Quetzalcoatl) was considered the inventor of hieroglyphs and hieroglyphs were known as "the word of the gods"[90], it is interesting that many of the plasma designs recorded on petroglyphs discussed in the previous chapter would later be adopted into writing systems around the world including by the Maya and Egyptians. Did this super solar storm not only lead to destruction but also the invention of writing? Is this why these messenger gods were all associated with the invention of writing? As noted in chapter 3 there is evidence that human creativity increases during periods of high solar activity thus this might explain the invention of writing at that time.

Thoth also had a female counterpart (or twin?) known as the goddess Seshat. She is usually represented in temple paintings wearing leopard skins. During major solar storms the sun is covered in sunspots thus the leopard skin is an ingenious way to represent a god associated with solar storms.

Above: Seshat (Courtesy Wikipedia)

In one depiction Seshat's spots were represented as stars suggestive of a meteor shower or storm. Seshat also wore an emblem on her head consisting of a seven-pointed star and a set of inverted cow's horns meant to represent a crescent moon.[91] (This crescent moon and star symbol appears all over the world associated with this cosmic catastrophe suggesting this configuration existed in the sky at the time of the destruction.)

Thoth is often portrayed with a green ibis head with long green and red feathers that flow from his head like a comet's tail. In fact, these colors are identical to depictions of Quetzalcoatl in Mexico.

Above: Thoth, the ibis-headed deity of Egypt. (See color version on back cover.)

Thus we see that Quetzalcoatl, Hermes and Thoth seem to be one-and-the-same. Yet Thoth adds an extra layer of meaning since he also is related to sunspots and thus solar flares. As noted previously, in January 2005 when Comet Machholz visited the Pleiades a major solar flare erupted 15 days later with the largest and fastest proton storm ever recorded. As noted previously, proton storms can cause severe bodily damage as well as genetic mutations. Could be the reason Quetzalcoatl's twin, Xolotl, was associated with deformity? Could the previous appearance of the green comet Machholz have coincided closely in time with the super solar flare at the beginning of the Younger Dryas event hence the symbolism of a green comet associated with sunspots and physical deformity?

For people on Earth, this super solar flare would have appeared as a great flash of light from the sun. Then minutes later the proton storm would have hit Earth's atmosphere and the high-energy plasma would have created all manner of lighting storms similar to being inside of a toy plasma globe. These lightning storms would have ignited the world's forests. According to one version of the Toba Indians' World Fire myth, the fire was indeed preceded by lightning.[92]

As night fell high-energy auroras would have appeared in the sky as vibrant, neon lights dancing across the sky in various designs including one that looked like a stick man with a bird's head. Is it any wonder the ancients thought the gods lived in the sky and hurled thunderbolts to destroy humanity?

Ancient myths suggest that not only were the forests ignited but also the water in lakes, ponds and the ocean reached boiling point. People who sought refuge in water were boiled to death except those who buried themselves in mud. On land only people who reached the safety of caves or dug holes in the ground were saved.

Could this be the reason that the great ice dams melted and released a deluge of fresh water into the oceans and a mass extinction occurred at that time? Could this also be the reason Quetzalcoatl, Hermes and Thoth were all associated with guiding souls to the 'underworld?' Does this portion of the myths suggest that caves and tunnels were the only safe places of refuge to escape the solar storm?

Interestingly, researcher Andrew Collins noted in his book *Beneath the Pyramids* that he recently discovered caves beneath the Great Pyramids of Egypt. The entrance to these caves was concealed behind a temple known as the Tomb of the Birds. It appears to have been a temple dedicated to Thoth since bird mummies were also found in another cemetery related to Thoth near Khemenu, a city dedicated to the worship of Thoth. This cemetery at Khemenu also featured extensive underground passageways.[93]

Also in Mexico archaeologists have recently discovered the entrance to a cave complex in front of the Temple of Quetzalcoatl at Teotihuacan, a pre-Columbian pyramid complex that was dedicated to the worship of Quetzalcoatl and his close associate Tlaloc. (Tlaloc was also associated with comets and destruction by a rain of fire as we will see in chapter 19.) Teotihuacan's great Pyramid of the Sun was also built over a cave and Hermes mother Maia gave birth to him in a cave.

Thus a clearer picture is emerging about the message that these ancient myths may encode. They suggest that the sun enters a new highly active period every 12,500 years that coincides with the return of the green comet Machholz as it passes near the Pleiades. During this time the sun, covered in sunspots, can influence weather on earth causing an increase in storm activity. During this period the sun can also emit super solar flares that are dangerous to life on Earth and can melt ice sheets, set forests ablaze and cause the ocean to boil. The only refuge is underground or in caves.

14. The Galactic Center and the Blue Star Kachina

The geologic evidence seems to support that there were both a super solar flare *and* a comet impact event around 10,500 BC. Yet how could such rare events occur simultaneously? Could both of these events have been caused by a third outside force: a massive eruption from the center of our galaxy? Physicist Paul LaViolette thinks that was precisely the case.

In his 1983 Ph.D. dissertation, Dr. Paul LaViolette argued that the megafaunal extinctions and other changes around the time of the Younger Dryas were caused by an eruption of cosmic rays from the center of our galaxy. This galactic superwave pushed large amounts of "cosmic dust and cometary debris into the solar system and triggered a period of elevated solar flare activity."[94]

Astronomers have witnessed core explosions known as gamma ray bursts from the centers of many galaxies. They usually appear blue in color. According to Dr. LaViolette the galactic core explosion from our own galaxy would appear to people on Earth as the appearance of a new bright blue star at the galactic center, which is located between the constellations Sagittarius and Scorpio. Depending on the intensity of the outburst it could have been visible during the day as well.

Above: Artist depiction of gamma ray burst from galactic center (Courtesy NASA. See color version on front cover.)

The Hopi Indians, who shared the Mesoamerican belief in a series of world ages called Suns, had a legend that the Fourth Sun would end and the Fifth Sun begin once a bright blue star was seen in the heavens. Known as the Blue Star Kachina, this was believed to also bring a "Day of Purification." Could this be a reference to a galactic core explosion?

Yet according to Aztec belief, the Fourth Sun ended and the Fifth Sun began in 1011 AD. Did something happen in the year 1011 AD that corresponded with Aztec prophecies about how and when the Fourth Sun would end?

In 1011 AD Chinese astronomers recorded the appearance of a "guest star" in their constellation known as the Rice Ladle. This constellation corresponds to our asterism called the Milk Dipper that is part of the constellation Sagittarius. As noted previously, the galactic center is located between Sagittarius and Scorpio. Thus was this "guest star" a minor eruption from the galactic center or perhaps simply a blue supernova or comet that appeared nearby but which the Aztecs confused for this prophetic blue star?

Interestingly, the Aztecs carved the Milk Dipper asterism into the flange of their famous Aztec Calendar Stone or Stone of the Fifth Sun.[95] This strongly suggests they thought this event was significant to the beginning of the Fifth Sun. They also carved a glyph that corresponded to the year 1011 AD as the year the Fifth Sun began. According to Aztec legends, the Fourth Sun ended with a catastrophe that included a flood and the sky falling.

Coincidentally, just three years later in 1014 AD the *Anglo Saxon Chronicles* described a tsunami hitting the British Isles:

> *"On the eve of St. Michael's day came the great seaflood, which spread wide over this land, and ran so far up as it never did before, overwhelming many towns, and an innumerable multitude of people."*

Astronomer Dallas Abbott of the Lamont-Doherty Earth Observatory at Columbia University discovered that this tsunami was likely caused by an impact of a comet fragment around the mid-Atlantic ridge and produced tsunamis that reached as far south as the Caribbean and South America. Thus, Aztec stories of the sky falling and a great flood are supported by scientific evidence. The fact that these events occurred so soon after the appearance of a guest star near or in the galactic center is the likely reason the Aztecs believed the Fourth Sun had ended and the Fifth Sun had begun. Yet apparently the Maya and Hopi did not agree that these events were severe enough to represent the end of a world age and continued to await the Fifth Sun.

This serves as a good reminder that the interpretation of ancient prophecies and myths is not simple and errors are quite easy to make. It does appear that the return of the comet Machholz is a good match for the return of

Quetzalcoatl as predicted in the Mayan book *Chilam Balam of Chumayel*. Two other green comets appeared during this period but none passed by the Pleiades nor did their orbital periods coincide with a known disaster in Earth's history. Thus comet Machholz seems to fit the bill.

Yet we must continue to look for other signs that corroborate these findings to see how well they coincide with the ancient myths. We must study other ancient prophecies and mythology to see if they, too, support these results.

Since the Maya believed that what happened in the past would recur in the future it might be instructive to find out what the Maya believed happened the last time their calendar ended. If these stories also contain references to super solar flares, comet impact events and the appearance of unusual stars then perhaps our previous interpretations will be further validated and we will be that much closer to understanding what the future may hold.

IV. What Happened the Last Time the Calendar Ended?

15. Decoding the Mayan Flood Myth

As demonstrated in the previous chapters, the Mayan short count calendar and its "prophecies" do seem to neatly coincide with natural 250-year cycles that influence everything from famines to human inventiveness. Does the Mayan long count calendar also coincide with a larger 5,000-year cycle of which modern science is currently unaware?

As noted previously, the Maya believed history was cyclical and what happened in the past would happen again in the future. Modern science believes much the same thing. Thus in order to determine the significance of the Maya ending their long count calendar on December 21, 2012 it would be good to ask the question, "What happened the last time the Mayan calendar ended?"

According to Mayan mythology Earth experienced a catastrophic flood near the end of the last Mayan calendar cycle. If one accepts the premise that mythology is astronomy in disguise then what are the possible astronomical underpinnings of the Mayan Flood Myth, which included the decapitation of a cosmic crocodile and resulting flood of blood? If any myth has an astronomical basis then surely it is this myth for it explicitly stated that the events it related all began in the sky.

The Mayan Flood Myth was recorded on a platform in Temple XIX at Palenque in Chiapas, Mexico. The myth was recorded in Mayan glyphs in the year 734 AD and discovered by archaeologists in 1999. According to Mayan scholar David Stuart who partially deciphered these glyphs, "the record of mythical…events recorded in these texts warrants their addition to the select group of highly important religious and historical documents from Palenque."[96]

The myth began with the date on which the events transpired: March 10, 3309 BC. On this date the myth related that a deity known as God GI was enthroned in the sky under the supervision of another deity named Yax Naah Itzamnaaj. Eleven years later it recorded that a cosmic caiman or crocodile was decapitated which resulted in a catastrophic flood of blood. Since it was the decapitation event that led to the flood, it is this event that I will decode first and attempt to find an astronomical explanation.

What was the cosmic crocodile?

According to Stuart, the glyphs that represented the cosmic crocodile included "two distinctive and unusual signs: a representation of a 'hunched' and seemingly headless human body and, below, a head of the creature [called] the 'Starry Deer Crocodile,' who seems a distinctive yet poorly understood aspect of the 'Celestial Monster' or 'Cosmic Serpent.'"[97]

In their 1982 book entitled *The Cosmic Serpent*, astronomers Bill Napier and Victor Clube argued that ancient references to cosmic serpents and dragons were, in actuality, references to comets.[98] Could Palenque's Cosmic Caiman or "Starry Deer Crocodile" represent a comet?

A comet consists of a head called a coma and a long tail. A crocodile also consists of a head and a body that merges into a long tail thus it would be easy to see why the ancient Maya would use such an animal to symbolize a comet.

According to Stuart, the crocodile heads in the aforementioned glyphs "each display the long-lashed 'star' eye and the long deer ear, also decorated by a 'star,' that readily identify it as the Starry Deer Crocodile."[99] Stuart also noted that "the Starry Deer Crocodile serves as the head variant of the day sign Lamat and also in the month patron for Yax, which in their standard forms are simply the 'star,' probably read **EK'**, 'star, planet.'"[100]

In other words, the Cosmic Crocodile had strong associations with stars/planets. Coincidentally, a comet does not begin growing its tail until it enters the inner solar system near Jupiter. Until that point it is indistinguishable from a star or planet. Perhaps the Maya referred to comets as "crocodile stars" once they grew their tails similarly to how the Chinese referred to comets as "long tailed pheasant stars."[101]

If Palenque's Cosmic Crocodile was, in fact, a comet then what sort of astronomical phenomenon could account for the decapitation event? A clue comes from the text itself that states the crocodile was decapitated eleven years after God GI was enthroned in the sky. It is known that the sun has an eleven-year sunspot cycle; i.e., every eleven years the sun enters an active phase wherein sunspots increase on its surface and solar flares and coronal mass ejections (CMEs) increase. Could a solar flare or CME be responsible for the decapitation event?

On April 20, 2007, NASA's STEREO-A probe was recording Comet Encke when the comet was hit by a massive coronal mass ejection from the sun. The CME ripped off the comet's tail leaving only its coma or head.[102] The CME *decapitated* the comet! This phenomenon is now referred to as a "tail disconnection event."[103] (Watch a time-lapse video of this event: http://apod.nasa.gov/apod/ap071003.html).

Interestingly, Stuart noted that the phrasing of the Palenque decapitation event was somewhat complex. It started with the word **CH'AK** meaning "to cut, chop something" followed by **U-BAAH** meaning "his/her/its self/body/head."[104] This suggests that the cosmic crocodile cut off its own body, which is precisely how the event would have appeared to an earth-based observer. A witness to the event would have simply seen the body and tail of the 'crocodile star' blown away leaving a disembodied head (coma) in the sky.

Is there any physical evidence that the sun was experiencing a heightened level of activity in 3300 BC? In fact, there is. Scientists have noted a Beryllium-10 spike in the Antarctic ice core that corresponds to 3300 BC[105]. Such spikes are associated with an increase in cosmic rays hitting the upper atmosphere, which can be caused by either supernovae or increased solar activity. Thus the physical evidence supports an interpretation that the ancient Maya recorded a tail disconnection event caused by a CME.

What was the flood of blood?

After the decapitation event, the myth recorded a flood of blood: "copiously flowed the blood of the one who raises the stream, the one who drills the fire."[106] Researchers have noted that crocodiles were associated with catastrophic floods throughout Mesoamerica.[107] The only way a comet could cause such a flood is if it or its fragments crashed into the ocean causing an impact tsunami. Evidence of four impact tsunamis dating to 3300 BC has, in fact, been discovered in the sedimentary record.[108] (Details later.) Yet how would a tail disconnection event lead to impacts in four separate oceans? The only way this could happen is if the comet fragmented into at least four large pieces.

When Comet Encke experienced its tail disconnection event the comet did not fragment and the tail later reformed. Is there any evidence that a CME could either cause or coincide with a fragmentation event?

The answer to this question came in August 2011 when Comet Elenin was struck by a CME. The comet immediately flared up and then astronomers noted it appeared to be breaking apart:

> *"Shortly after the coronal mass ejection the comet flared up and you could see some beautiful details in the tail, with the tail was twisting about in the solar wind. But shortly after that Earth- bound amateurs reported a huge decrease in the intensity of the comet. We think it may presage a falling apart of the comet."*[109]

Currently no physics model can explain how a CME can fragment a comet thus scientists doubt the CME caused the breakup and believe that, instead, it was caused by the sun's gravitational pull and the CME just happened to hit at the same time. Regardless, to an eyewitness on earth the comet's tail being ripped off followed by a fragmentation that led to impacts and mega-tsunamis would have seemed connected regardless of the true physics behind the event. (Interestingly, another Mesoamerican crocodile known as Cipactli was always represented as the disembodied head of a crocodile missing its lower jaw. Could this missing lower jaw have been meant to represent the fragmentation of the comet nucleus?)

The fact that a CME was involved in this event likely explains the description of this flood as being "a flood of blood." When a CME hits earth it can cause the sky to turn blood red via intense auroras. For instance, in 1859 during the strongest solar storm in recorded history known as the Carrington Event, red auroras were seen as far south as the Caribbean. The *New York Times* noted, "At that time almost the whole southern heavens were in a livid red flame, brightest still in the southeast and southwest." The *New York Herald* reported that the sky appeared "blood red."[110] The *Sydney Morning Herald* noted, "the spectacle presented by the southern heavens at this time was very impressive, the sky being of a deep, blood-red colour."[111] Interestingly, the ancient Greeks referred to this type of aurora as 'red rain.'[112]

Coincidentally, immediately preceding the red auroras, exploding meteors were also reported in Australian eyewitness accounts:

> "...a brilliant meteor was seen to shoot through the sky...and when near the horizon, burst like a rocket. Almost immediately afterwards the rays of an aurora Australis were most brilliantly visible in the N.E."

> "A very brilliant meteor was seen towards the south, which fell in a curve from about 45 deg. elevation, standing to the eastward. Almost

> *immediately following this the glancing rays of a vivid aurora shot up the sky, at first more fully developed to the west, but afterwards stretching across the whole of the south from the hills to the sea."*[113]

Interestingly, these accounts give a close approximation for the events that were recorded in Mayan Flood Myth: first, meteor impact(s) followed by the sky turning blood red.

Yet this flood of blood may not have been purely a flood of red auroral light in the sky. A phenomenon known as blood rain has consistently been associated with comets and meteors throughout the ages. For instance, astronomers believe an impact event was the cause of the severe weather event of 536-541 AD in which temperatures plummeted across the globe. Eyewitness accounts from this time period record,

> "In the year of grace 541, there appeared a comet in Gaul, so vast that the whole sky seemed on fire. In the same year there dropped real blood from the clouds, and about the same time...a dreadful mortality ensued."[114]

This red rain is thought to be the result of dust-laded rain although other theories exist.[115] Yet the flood recorded in this Mayan myth was much more devastating and catastrophic than a simple flood of red auroral light and red rain. This flood was said to have brought one world age to an end. As suggested previously, the only way a comet could have caused a flood is if a sizeable fragment crashed into the ocean creating an impact tsunami. Coincidentally, evidence suggests earth really did experience multiple high-energy mega-tsunamis in the year 3300 BC.

Mayan flood caused by impact mega-tsunami?

Edward Bryant in his book *Tsunami: The Underrated Hazard*, found evidence in southeastern Australia of "six separate tsunami events...over the past 8,000 years, with peaks at 7500 B.C., 5000 B.C., **3300 B.C.**, 500-2000 B.C., **A.D. 500**, and A.D. 1500."[116] He also noted in another paper that the "North Atlantic region has additional evidence for at least seven major tsunami...[that] occurred in 60 BC, 218-216 BC, 1763 BC, 1862 BC, 2153 BC, **3309 BC**, and 4000-5000 BC."[117] He also noted that three more tsunami events happened in the northern British Isles in "**AD 500**, 3250-3150 BC, and **3300 BC**."[118] Additionally, Baille has noted that the 3200 BC event was "a prime candidate of an impact event that affected more than one ocean."

The hypothesis that the flood recorded in the Mayan Flood Myth was caused by an impact event is further supported by an account of the same event in the *Chilam Balam of Chumayel*. This Mayan book of prophecy and history described the events surrounding the flood that ended the last age. These descriptions sound remarkably like an eyewitness account of an impact event:

> *Then it was that fire descended, then the rope descended, then rocks and trees descended. Then came the beating of <things> with wood and stone....After that the fatherless ones, the miserable ones, and those without husbands were all pierced through; they were alive though they had no hearts. Then they were buried in the sands, in the sea. There would be a sudden rush of water... Then the sky would fall, it would fall down upon the earth, when the four gods, the four Bacabs, were set up, who brought about the destruction of the world.*[119]

Another version of this event was recorded in the *Chilam Balam of Mani*:

> ...the days and night that fell without order, and pain was felt throughout the land....[Ah Mesencab] turned the sky and the Peten upside down, and...there was a great cataclysm, and the ages ended with a flood....fire, stones, and clubs came down...After that the evil sons and daughters were buried, although alive [they had no hearts], and those who were on the beach were buried between the waves of the sea....an avalanche of water came and...everything came to an end. It was said that four gods, four Bacabs, were the ones who destroyed the earth.[120]

Any doubt as to the true nature of the Bacabs is cleared up in a passage from the *Chilam Balam of Tizimin* that noted, "The four Bacabs slide to earth on the back of a green rainbow. One by one the stars fall."[121] Clearly the Bacabs were seen as meteors. The "green rainbow" is likely a reference to the green color many meteors emit when they burn up in the atmosphere. The fact that there were four Bacabs (meteors) coincides nicely with the evidence that there were four mega-tsunamis in four separate oceans around 3300 BC.

The order of events listed in these Mayan "mythological" accounts coincide well with the eyewitness accounts from the Tunguska event, one of only three known witnessed impact events in the last 100 years. The Tunguska event took place in the year 1908 in Russian Siberia. The meteor exploded before hitting the ground creating an airburst similar to that of a nuclear bomb. The eyewitness accounts match perfectly to the effects of nuclear explosions as recorded in film footage from nuclear tests in the 1940s and 50s. For instance, a nuclear airburst will first create a superheated blast of hurricane-force winds followed by a secondary blast of super-hurricane force winds that will blow down trees and structures. According to the Centers for Disease Control:

> *"In a nuclear blast, injury or death may occur as a result of the blast itself or as a result of debris thrown from the blast. People may experience moderate to severe skin burns, depending on their distance from the blast site. Those who look directly at the blast could experience eye damage ranging from temporary blindness to severe burns on the retina."*[122]

One eyewitness account from forty miles of the epicenter of the Tunguska impact noted:

> *the sky split in two and fire appeared high and wide over the forest…The split in the sky grew larger, and the entire northern side was covered with fire. At that moment I became so hot that I couldn't bear it, as if my shirt was on fire; from the northern side, where the fire was, came strong heat. I wanted to tear off my shirt and throw it down, but then the sky shut closed, and a strong thump sounded, and I was thrown a few metres. I lost my senses for a moment, but then my wife ran out and led me to the house. After that such noise came, as if rocks were falling or cannons were firing, the earth shook, and when I was on the ground, I pressed my head down, fearing rocks would smash it. When the sky opened up, hot wind raced between the houses, like from cannons, which left traces in the ground like pathways, and it damaged some crops. Later we saw that many windows were shattered, and in the barn a part of the iron lock snapped.*[123]

Another account from tribal members who lived in the area noted:

We had a hut by the river with my brother Chekaren. We were sleeping. Suddenly we both woke up at the same time. Somebody shoved us. We heard whistling and felt strong wind. Chekaren said, 'Can you hear all those birds flying overhead?' We were both in the hut, couldn't see what was going on outside. Suddenly, I got shoved again, this time so hard I fell into the fire. I got scared. Chekaren got scared too. We started crying out for father, mother, brother, but no one answered. There was noise beyond the hut, we could hear trees falling down. Chekaren and I got out of our sleeping bags and wanted to run out, but then the thunder struck. This was the first thunder. The Earth began to move and rock, wind hit our hut and knocked it over. My body was pushed down by sticks, but my head was in the clear. Then I saw a wonder: trees were falling, the branches were on fire, it became mighty bright, how can I say this, as if there was a second sun, my eyes were hurting, I even closed them. It was like what the Russians call lightning. And immediately there was a loud thunderclap. This was the second thunder. The morning was sunny, there were no clouds, our Sun was shining brightly as usual, and suddenly there came a second one!

The primary difference between the Mayan accounts and Tunguska accounts is the Tunguska accounts lacked the "sudden rush of water" and "avalanche of water" referred to in the Mayan accounts since the event took place over land and not water. Due to the date of the event it is believed the Tunguska event was caused by meteors that were part of the Taurid meteor stream produced by fragments of Comet Encke.

A Cycle of Cosmic Catastrophes?

The Mayan Flood Myth was recorded in Palenque's Temple XIX, which was dedicated on January 14, 734 AD. Yet this was likely a re-dedication of a rebuilt structure, the previous temple having been destroyed by invaders. It is unknown when the original temple was built but an inscription noted the dedication of an *okib* (the platform on which the inscriptions appear) was made in 561 AD. Why would this platform with its 3500 year-old flood myth be constructed at this time? Could a similar celestial event have occurred which reminded the Mayan priests of this ancient myth and thus led to its revival?

In fact, in March 536 A.D. a major climactic event occurred worldwide which dimmed the sun, caused summer to turn to winter, and caused crops to fail. Originally thought to have been the result of a volcanic eruption it is now thought the event resulted from "multiple comet impacts."[124] The fact that this event occurred at the beginning of March[125] is eerily similar to the Mayan Flood Myth which began with the enthronement of God GI on March 10, 3309 BC. Perhaps the appearance of a comet that broke up and crashed into the ocean causing worldwide haze that dimmed the sun and floods resulting from impact tsunamis made the priests remember these old myths and revived them at Palenque in 561 A.D.?

In fact, scientists believe at least two comet fragments crashed into two separate bodies of water during this event. One fragment "roughly 640 metres wide slammed into the Gulf of Carpentaria in Australia, and the other…smaller object crashed into the North Sea near Norway."[126] These led to mega-tsunamis in two of the planet's oceans. In fact, researchers noted that of the "'six separate [Australian] tsunami events that can be recognized over the last 8000 years'…two dates stand out, namely 5250 cal. Yr BP (3300

BC) and 1450 cal. Yr BP (AD 500)"[127] because these same dates can be found over and over again in publications devoted to tsunami research. Interestingly, researchers have noted that the peak of the A.D. 500 tsunami event corresponded "with a clustering of meteor sightings that is believed by astronomers to be one of the most significant over this time span...[and is] associated with the Taurid complex"[128] created by Comet Encke.

Thus it seems clear that the 500 A.D. event was so similar to the 3300 BC event that it likely revived the memory of the older 3300 BC event, which then inspired the Maya to create a hieroglyphic text of this earlier catastrophe.

Just as in the 500 AD event[129], the Earth experienced rapid global cooling in the 3300 BC event as well.[130] (Coincidentally, the famous Otzi the Ice Man who was discovered in the Alps frozen to death died around 3300 BC and his stomach contents showed this occurred sometime in Spring making him a likely victim of this rapid global cooling.) Victor Clube and Bill Napier, authors of *The Cosmic Serpent*, theorized in their second book, *The Cosmic Winter*, that comet impact events would lead to a global winter much like a nuclear winter as dust from the impacts would block out the sun. Thus the similarities between the 3300 BC event and 500 AD event likely explain why the 3300 BC event was recorded at Palenque so soon after the 500 AD event.

Supernova or Galactic Core Explosion?

So far we have discussed the possible astronomical basis of the "main event" recorded in the Mayan Flood Myth; namely, the flood caused by multiple meteor impacts into the world's oceans. Yet this was not the first event mentioned in the myth.

The hieroglyphic text begins with the enthronement of God GI in the heavens on March 10, 3309 BC, overseen by a deity named Yax Naah Itzamnaaj. Curiously, the myths surrounding God GI have him being born and enthroned multiple times. This has confused scholars but makes sense when one realizes that his enthronement in the sky is best explained as the appearance of a supernova in the sky. Supernova can brighten, becoming visible, and dim, becoming invisible, multiple times before they finally explode. Thus, GI's multiple births become explicable via an astronomical interpretation.

The fact that God GI was enthroned on March 10, 3309 BC suggests he was not in the sky before this date. Most stars are always in the sky night after night thus they do not "come to power." They are simply always there. Only a supernova appears out of nowhere and takes its position in the sky, i.e., is "enthroned." The fact that supernovae are usually so bright they are even visible during daylight hours is likely another reason they are said to be "enthroned," since they are the "king" of the stars during their short reign in the sky.

Is there any physical evidence for a supernova in 3300 BC? In fact, there is. Scientists have noted that a Beryllium-10 spike appears in the east Antarctic ice core record around the year 3300 BC. Beryllium-10 spikes are associated with increased cosmic rays reaching earth. This has been shown to have two causes: increased solar activity and supernova outbursts.

As was noted previously, the decapitation event is consistent with a tail disconnection event caused when a coronal mass ejection slams into a comet. Coronal mass ejections occur during periods of heightened solar activity thus the Mayan Flood Myth suggests these events took place during such a period. This, alone, could explain the Beryllium-10 spike in the ice core record. Yet if God GI was really a supernova then this could also help explain the spike in Beryllium-10.

What are the odds that a supernova, super solar storm, and comet impact event would all happen so closely in time? Could there be some other underlying cause to all of these rare events just as there was for the 10,500 BC event discussed in Chapter 14?

Once again, just like with the 10,500 BC event, a galactic core explosion and associated superwave appear to be the root cause behind these rare events. Physicist Paul LaViolette, Ph.D. noted in his book *Earth Under Fire* that the Beryllium-10 spike in 3300 BC was likely the result of a minor Magnitude 1 superwave.[131] Though not as severe as the Magnitude 4 galactic superwave that struck the solar system in 10,500 BC, this superwave was still able to pack a powerful punch. It was able to obliterate comets in the Oort cloud in the outer reaches of the solar system and push this dust, gas and debris into the inner solar system where it collided with the earth and sun. The massive amount of dust and debris falling into the sun caused it to become more active shooting off super solar flares and coronal mass ejections. One of these superflares or CMEs caused a tail disconnection event as well as a violent outgassing of the comet that led to a fragmentation. Four large fragments then slammed into four of the world's oceans sending mega-tsunami with wave heights likely 1000 feet or more racing towards shore.

The shock wave produced by these meteor impacts would have reached land before the tsunami wave in the form of greater-than-hurricane-force winds. These winds would have been so hot that most organic matter would have burst into flames. A second blast wave would have soon followed. Any survivors of the initial blast would have been pelted by a rain of rocks, trees and other debris. Soon afterwards a mountain of water would have appeared and crashed down on any remaining survivors. The fact that eyewitness accounts of these events were preserved so accurately within Mayan religious texts proves that, miraculously, some people who witnessed these events actually survived them!

Additionally, the appearance of God GI in the heavens may have been an eyewitness account of the blue 'star' that would have appeared in the galactic center when the light from this eruption reached an observer on earth. When the tail disconnection event and impact events happened eleven years later the astronomer-priests may have assumed these events were related just as the Aztecs did four thousand years later for the 1011 AD supernova and 1014 AD impact events discussed in Chapters 13 & 14.

The 3300 BC event also seems to coincide with the birth or rebirth of the Taurid meteor stream. Astronomer Bill Napier has noted, "The main part of the current [Taurid] meteoroid system appears to have developed five to 20,000 years ago."[132] Thus it is likely that the event in 3300 BC, five thousand years ago, could have created or significantly added to the current Taurid meteoroid complex, which would have devastating consequences for civilization over the next 5,000 years.

Yax Naah Itzamnaaj & the Constellation Draco

There is one final deity associated with these events: Yax Naah Itzamnaaj. The hieroglyphic text notes that he oversaw the enthronement of God GI.

Itzamna was one of the most ancient gods whose myths were very reminiscent of those told about Quetzalcoatl, the sky serpent. Itzamna's name has been interpreted to mean "lizard house" where *itzam* means "lizard" and *na* means "house." House and/or mansion were common terms used by cultures around the world to refer to a constellation. One constellation has been represented as both a lizard and serpent around the world: Draco. Could Itzamna be associated with the constellation Draco?

One researcher noted, "Itzamnaaj a.k.a. 'God D,' [was] a high-ranking, wrinkled Old God, ubiquitous in Maya art, usually ruling over other gods. Occasionally…God D [appeared] as a serpent-head."[133] In Mayan mythology, Itzamna was married to Ix Chel who was depicted as having a serpent on her head, carrying a water jug, usually overturned pouring out water.

The Little Dipper asterism to the Maya was known as the "water jug," *xam*, which pours out virgin water.[134] If Ix Chel represented the Little Dipper then it is likely that Itzamna represented the constellation Draco which is "married" to the Little Dipper in the night sky since they endlessly rotate around each other, even passing ownership of the North star between one another due to precession. Draco sits on top of the Little Dipper just as depictions of Ix Chel represent.

Since Draco was a circumpolar constellation it was visible year round unlike other constellations that dip below the horizon for months at a time; thus, it was an appropriate, ever-present "deity" to rule over the other deities, i.e., comets, supernovae and constellations. More importantly, due to precession of the equinoxes, Draco was home to the North Star, Thuban, in 3300 BC. In Mesoamerican artwork stars were often depicted as eyes. Thus the North Star, which never sets, could easily have been seen as an all-seeing-eye, an omnipotent overseer of all celestial events.

Since Draco was home to the North Star which is always visible, never sets and is the center point around which all the other stars and constellations rotated, this would explain why he was said to have overseen the events of 3300 BC.

What about the title *Yax Naah* he is given in this hieroglyphic text? *Yax* means "green" but also "first." *Naah* means house. Combined they likely mean something like "the original" Itzamna. This title was likely meant to distinguish him from the later incarnations of Itzamna that conflated him with Quetzalcoatl, which we have seen was clearly a comet not a constellation. (This cometary version of Itzamna will be seen in the next chapter, "Decoding the Mayan Blowgunner Vase.")

Conclusions

Based on the above interpretations, it seems likely that on March 10, 3309 BC the blue light from a galactic core explosion arrived at earth appearing like a new blue star in the sky. The "enthronement" of this new star was "overseen" by the constellation Draco which was home to the North Star, Thuban. This explosion pushed in dust and comets into the inner solar system causing the sun to become more active spawning superflares and coronal mass ejections. One such CME slammed into a comet, ripping its tail off in a tail detachment event, and fragmenting the comet. The CME also slammed into earth causing blood red auroras to overtake the world's skies.

Soon afterwards four large fragments of the comet, burning bright green as they burned in the atmosphere, crashed into four separate oceans spawning mega-tsunamis. The initial blast wave created super hurricane force winds that uprooted and shredded trees for thousands of kilometers. Then the mega-tsunami, an avalanche of water, rushed inland for miles destroying everything in its path then washed it all back out to sea. The dust and debris would blot out the sun for two years or more. Survivors would tell how a crocodile star was decapitated, flooded the world with blood, and caused the sky to fall bringing about the end of one world age.

16. Decoding the Mayan Blowgunner Vase

As mentioned previously, the Mayan Flood Myth recorded the "decapitation" of a comet and impact of its fragments into four oceans causing worldwide mega-tsunamis. The "myth" recorded that this decapitation event happened eleven years after the initial "enthronement" or appearance of a new star in the sky around 3309 BC. Evidence for these events has been found in both the sedimentary and ice core records dated to 3300 BC providing physical evidence that the Mayan Flood "Myth" was more likely an eyewitness account of actual events.

The inclusion of the eleven-year span of time after the "enthronement" suggests the "decapitation" event was caused by the Sun. The Sun is known to have an eleven-year cycle. Every eleven years the Sun becomes more active, sunspots form on its surface, and solar flares and coronal mass ejections become more frequent. Could the Maya have known about this eleven-year sunspot cycle and encoded it in this myth?

A Mayan vase known as the Blowgunner Vase suggests this is the case. This vase likely recorded the same event as the Mayan Flood Myth. It featured a character known as *Jun Ahaw*, "One Lord" or "One Sun," shooting *Itzam Yeh*, the Celestial Bird, with a blowgun and causing the bird to "descend from the sky."[135]

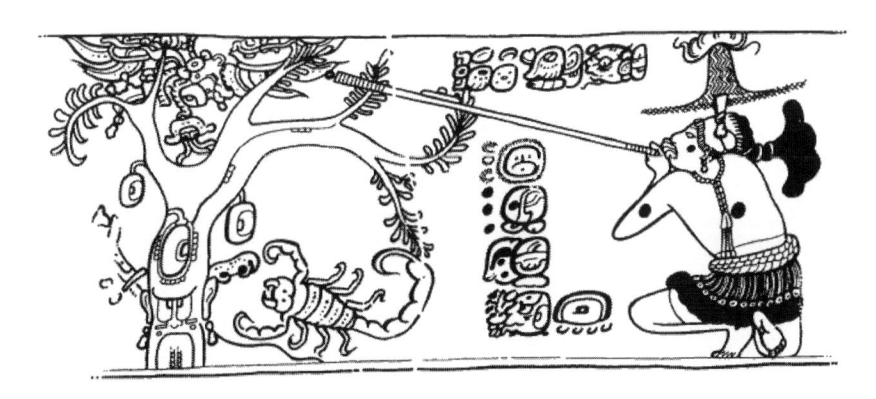

Above: Detail of the Blowgunner Vase showing Jun Ahaw using a blowgun to shoot down the Celestial Bird. Notice the spots on the body of Jun Ahaw, "One Sun."

The Celestial Bird was represented as a Quetzal. As noted in chapter 8, "Comet Machholz and the Return of Kukulkan," the Quetzal was a species of bird from southern Mexico that had very long tail feathers. A bird that flew across the sky with long tail feathers was an appropriate symbol for a comet. As noted previously, the Chinese referred to one specific type of comet as a "long tailed pheasant star"[136] showing that birds with long tail feathers were, indeed, associated with comets in other cultures as well. (As I will show later this Chinese "long-tailed pheasant star" and the Mayan "Celestial Bird" were likely the same comet.)

The Mayan Blowgunner Vase also supports the idea that the Sun was responsible for the comet breakup and subsequent impact event. For instance, the blowgunner Jun Ahaw or "One Sun" had three spots on his body. Thus he likely represented the Sun during a solar maximum when sunspot activity was at its peak. The act of using a blowgun to shoot a Celestial Bird out of the sky was a good metaphor for a coronal mass ejection that caused the comet to fragment and impact the earth. The glyphs on the vase read "he descends (from) the sky" which further supports the idea that the Celestial Bird, or comet, was knocked from the sky by this action.

Above: Mayan Blowgunner Vase (Photo by Justin Kerr)

Yet a coronal mass ejection is not visible to someone on earth thus how would the Maya have known the sun was responsible for the tail disconnection event? First, naked-eye observations of sunspots have been recorded throughout history.[137] They are especially visible at sunrise and sunset when the apparent size of the sun is much larger than at midday. A hazy or cloudy day can help screen the bright glare of the sun allowing the solar disc to be viewed more easily. Under these conditions sunspots are readily seen by the naked eye.

Solar flares can also be witnessed by the naked eye under the same conditions. To the naked eye they will appear as bright flashes of light much brighter than the surrounding solar disc. These are called White-Light-Flares.[138] British astronomer Richard Carrington witnessed the largest solar storm in recorded history in September 1859 and noted the bright spots on the sun lasted for several minutes and were in the vicinity of the dark sunspots.[139] Carrington connected these bright spots to the blood red auroras that occurred the next night and suspected a solar-terrestrial connection.[140] Thus it is quite likely the Maya also made a connection between a White Light Flare during the day followed by a tail detachment and fragmentation event the next night and represented it as the figure of Jun Ahaw, covered in spots, shooting down the Celestial Bird.

Could the events depicted on the Mayan Blowgunner vase be the same as those recorded in the Mayan Flood Myth? Any doubts about whether the Celestial Bird and Cosmic Crocodile are related are removed by a sculpture at the site of Izapa in Chiapas, Mexico. Palenque, the site where the Mayan Flood Myth was recorded on a hieroglyphic platform, is also located in Chiapas. The sculpture, or stela, at Izapa showed the Celestial Bird in a tree formed by the body of a crocodile.

Above: Stela 25 from Izapa in Chiapas, Mexico. (Courtesy Wikipedia)

Another stela, stela 2, from Izapa showed the Celestial Bird diving towards Earth similarly to how the hieroglyphic text on the Mayan Blowgunner Vase recorded that the Celestial Bird "descended from the sky."

Above: Stela 2 from Izapa in Chiapas, Mexico (Courtesy Wikipedia)

As noted in chapter 10, "Quetzalcoatl & Hermes: Cosmic Messengers," the Greek god Hermes was associated with both a comet and the Sun. An old illustration of Hermes is remarkably similar to the Izapa stela 2 and showed the "bird of Hermes" descending above a tree made not from a Cosmic Crocodile but a two-headed dragon. It is

114

as if the bird is splitting the dragon in two. The scene is watched over by both the Sun and the crescent Moon.

335. THE BIRD OF HERMES AND THE ALCHEMIC DRAGON WITH TWO HEADS, SHOWING THE ANIMATION OF THE WORK BY CELESTIAL INFLUENCE
Elias Ashmole, *Theatrum chemicum Britannicum* (London, 1652).

Finally, the Blowgunner Vase prominently featured a serpent that overwatched the events depicted. As noted in the previous chapter, the events that preceded the flood were overwatched by Itzamna who likely represented the constellation Draco. This serpent on the Blowgunner Vase likely represents Draco as well providing another connection between the Mayan Flood Myth and the Blowgunner Vase.

If the serpent represented the constellation Draco then the scorpion likely represented the constellation Scorpio. This suggests the comet was in the constellation Scorpio when it was hit by the coronal mass ejection. Coincidentally, the Chinese associated a blue-green dragon with the constellation Scorpio. As has been noted before, dragons were simply another way of representing comets. Thus it appears that both the Maya and Chinese associated a blue-green comet with the constellation Scorpio.

Taking into account all of the previous information, it appears there is substantial evidence among ancient myths supporting the hypothesis that a comet was hit by a super solar flare or coronal mass ejection causing it to fragment. The evidence also supports that some of these fragments slammed into Earth's oceans leading to mega-tsunamis that undoubtedly destroyed many coastal civilizations at that time.

Since this was a global event is there any evidence that other cultures around the world encoded this event into their myths and legends. In fact, there is which we will explore in the next section. We will also learn about the only prophecy that specifically mentions December 21, 2012 and, unfortunately, it sounds a lot like an impact event.

V. Comet Catastrophe

17. Rahu and Ketu: A Hindu Account

As noted previously, Mayan mythology appears to accurately recount a catastrophic comet fragmentation and impact event that occurred around 3300 BC. According to these myths it appears that a super solar flare or coronal mass ejection was responsible for the fragmentation of the comet which led to four large fragments impacting the Earth's oceans creating mega-tsunamis that devastated coastal civilizations of the time.

Since this was a global catastrophe, is there any evidence of this event recorded in the myths and legends of other cultures around the globe? The Maya referred to this comet as a Cosmic Crocodile or a Celestial Bird thus it is likely the myths of other cultures encoded this comet in similarly fantastical ways. Is there any evidence for this? In fact, there is.

This same story appears to have been recorded in Hindu mythology as well. As researcher Bob Kobres noted in his research about bird-comet connections:

> *"The bird-comet connection is even more obvious in the [Hindu epic] the MAHABHARATA which describes a fierce fowl with but one wing, one eye, and one leg, hovering in the night sky. As this bird 'screams' and 'vomits blood,' 'All the quarters of the earth, being overwhelmed by showers of dust, look inauspicious. Fierce clouds, portentous of danger, drop bloody showers during the night. Rahu of fierce deeds is also, O monarch, afflicting the constellation Kirtika (Pleiades). Rough winds, portending fierce danger, are constantly blowing.'"*[141]

Interestingly, this bird-comet is associated with blood rain and vomited blood just as the Crocodile Star or Cosmic Crocodile from the Mayan Flood Myth discussed previously. Also interestingly, Kobres noted that Rahu was the "demon of eclipse, which originally had four arms and a tail that was severed by Vishnu to become Ketu (comet)."[142] Rahu was referred to as the head of the dragon and Ketu was called the tail of the dragon which "gave birth to comets and meteors."[143] Thus if there were any doubts about the interpretation of the Cosmic Crocodile as a comet there can be no such doubts about Rahu-Ketu for the myths state explicitly that this is the case.

According to Wikipedia:

In Hindu tradition, Rahu is a cut-off head of an asura, that swallows the sun or the moon causing eclipses. He is depicted in art as a serpent with no body riding a chariot drawn by eight black horses... Various names assigned to Rahu in Vedic texts — the chief, the advisor of the demons, the minister of the demons, ever-angry, the tormentor, bitter enemy of the luminaries, lord of illusions, one who frightens the Sun, the one who makes the Moon lusterless...Rahu is known as the "artificial sun"[144]

The origins of Rahu and Ketu sound very reminiscent of the Cosmic Crocodile myth. According to Hindu accounts, Vishnu threw his Sudarshan Chakra at Swarbhanu (Rahu) and cut him in half with the head being called Rahu and the body being called Ketu. Vishnu is believed by scholars to be an ancient Sun god. According to Hindu mythology Sudarshan Chakra was created from Sun "dust" after the Sun was dimmed.[145] In other words, Sudarshan Chakra was considered to be a piece of the sun thus Vishnu, a sun god, throwing Sudarshan Chakra, a piece of the sun, appears to represent a coronal mass ejection.

Above: Vishnu holds the Sudarshan Chakra disc in one hand. (Brooklyn Museum)

This Hindu story appears to support Paul LaViolette's galactic superwave theory discussed in chapter 14, "The Galactic Center and the Blue Star Kachina," which argued that eruptions from the galactic core, upon reaching the outer solar system, would vaporize comets in the Oort cloud and push this mass of dust and debris inward where it would fall onto the Sun, dimming the Sun and causing it to enter an active phase (called a T Tauri phase). During this active phase the sun would emit super solar flares and coronal mass ejections. Thus the sun dimming and then emitting solar flares and CMEs is consistent with the Hindu account of the Sudarshan Chakra (coronal mass ejection) forming after the sun was dimmed.

The fact that Rahu was known as the artificial sun is reminiscent of the eyewitness account from Tunguska that noted the meteor was like a second sun. The fact that Rahu "makes the Moon lusterless," is the "bitter enemy of the luminaries," and is associated with both solar and lunar eclipses on "unusual days" likely resulted from the immense amount of dust thrown into the atmosphere from an impact event that blocked out the light from the Sun and Moon. This is reminiscent of the written records associated with the 536 AD event where the Sun and Moon were blotted out for eighteen months.

Thus, once again we have an ancient story of a comet whose tail was severed giving birth to comets and meteors and then vomiting blood just like in the Mayan Flood Myth.

Curiously, the fact that Rahu had four arms is similar to the Chinese design for the "long-tailed pheasant star." In Carl Sagan's book *Comet*, he noted that in a Chinese comet atlas this particular comet was shaped like a swastika.

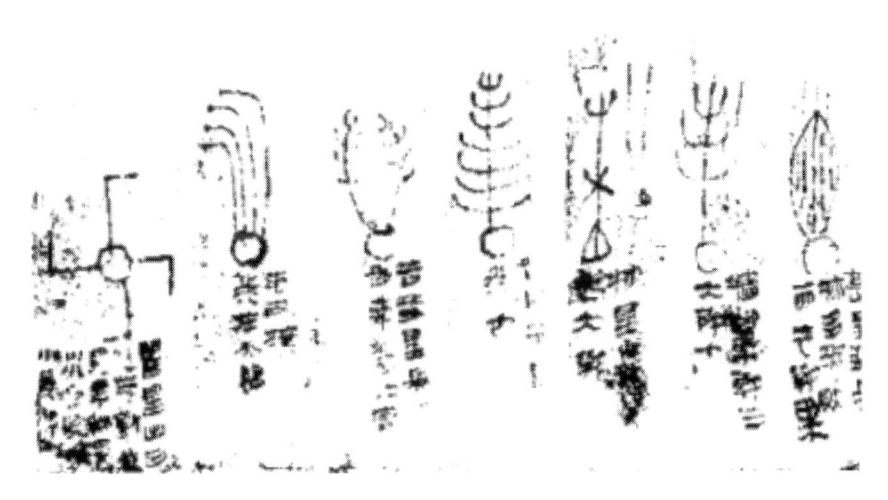

Above: The swastika-shaped comet was referred to as a "long-tailed pheasant star."

Other researchers have noted that the only way a comet could have the appearance of a swastika was if an observer on earth was looking at it head-on. We normally see a side view of comets as they pass by Earth with their two or more tails stretched out behind them. But if the comet headed directly for Earth we would see the tails arranged in a swastika configuration. Researchers have also noted that comet Encke, the same comet that was decapitated in 2007 and is the parent of the Taurid meteor stream, is the one comet whose orbit makes it possible to give a radial or head-on view like this to observers on Earth.

Even more interesting, Kobres noted that in the aforementioned Hindu story Rahu was afflicting Kirtika, the Pleiades, during the month of Karttika, which corresponds to the latter half of October through mid November. The Taurid meteor shower takes place during October and November and appears to emanate from the Pleiades:

> "the demon is here darkening Kirtika (the Pleiades) in the month of Karttika (latter half of October, through mid November), for the tale goes on to relate that, '. . . in course of the same month both the Moon and the Sun have undergone eclipses on the thirteenth days from the day of the first lunation. The Sun and the Moon therefore, by undergoing eclipses on unusual days, will cause a great slaughter of the creatures of the earth. Meteors, effulgent like Indra's thunder-bolt, fall with loud hisses . . . People, for meeting together, coming out of their houses with lighted brands, have still to encounter a thick gloom all round . . . From the mountains of Kailasa and Mandara and Himavat thousands of explosions are heard and thousands of summits are tumbling down . . . Fierce winds charged with pointed pebbles are blowing, crushing mighty trees. In villages and towns trees, ordinary and sacred, are falling down, crushed by mighty winds and struck by lightning.'"

It seems very clear from these descriptions that the celestial bird in this story was a comet that had broken apart and whose fragments rained down upon India causing all manner of destruction.

Interestingly, both Rahu and the Cosmic Crocodile were associated with spirals. This further associates them with the swastika-shaped comet. As stated previously, the only way an observer on Earth could see a swastika-shaped comet is if it were headed directly towards them. As this comet rotated the swastika arms would form a spiral in the sky.

Above: Notice the spirals in the eyes and elsewhere on this statue of Rahu. (©Kriangsak Hongsuwanwattana. See color version on back cover.)

Above: Two Cosmic Crocodiles with spiral, curly-q designs above or near their eyes.

Quetzalcoatl, the Feathered Serpent, was also associated with spirals. Sculptures of Quetzalcoatl at Teotihuacan and Chichen Itza both featured spirals on the side of the serpent's head. This makes it clear that the Celestial Bird, Cosmic Crocodile and Feathered Serpent were different ways to represent the same comet.

*Above: Quetzalcoatl sculpture from Teotihuacan featuring spiral design.
(Courtesy Wikipedia)*

*Above: Quetzalcoatl sculpture from Chichen Itza featuring spiral design
(Courtesy Wikipedia)*

One final legend surrounding Rahu sounds remarkably like a comet that breaks up into multiple pieces in the atmosphere. As Wikipedia notes,

> *"In the Tibetan Buddhist tradition, Rahu (or Rahula)...is usually depicted with nine heads and a thousand eyes all over his dark-colored body. In his four arms he holds a bow and arrow, and often a lasso and victory banner. He is wrathful in appearance, ablaze with fire, and his lower body has the form of a snake. Rahula is...a class of deities associated with the heavenly bodies."*[146]

Rahu "ablaze with fire, and his lower body has the form of a snake" could provide no better description of a meteor as it burns in the atmosphere leaving a long smoky tail trailing behind. His nine heads would be the resulting nine fragments as the meteor broke apart. The thousand eyes would be the innumerable meteorites that would accompany the nine larger fragments looking like the glowing eyes of animals in the night sky.

It now seems clear that the symbols used to encode these myths are all consistent with the interpretation that a bird-like, swastika-shaped comet appeared in the sky. As it rotated the arms of the swastika formed a spiral. An eruption from the sun ripped off these arms and tails and likely caused the comet to fragment. Several of these fragments "descended from the sky," burning bright green as they entered the atmosphere. These fragments impacted multiple oceans causing mega-tsunamis that destroyed coastal settlements. The survivors recorded these events in their myths and legends as well as their artwork.

Now let us take a look at some other myths from around the world that also recorded this event and see what additional details can be discovered.

18. Samson: A Biblical Account

The Hindu story of Rahu and the Mayan story of the Celestial Bird and Cosmic Crocodile were not the only ancient myths that encoded this comet fragmentation and impact event. Interestingly, the story of Samson in the Bible also appears to encode this same event. In this story, Samson's hair was cut which caused him to lose his strength. He was then enslaved and blinded and later destroyed the pillars holding up the roof of the Philistine's temple.

If Samson represented a comet then the cutting of Samson's long hair was equivalent to a tail detachment event in which a comet loses its long tail. *Comet*, in actuality, means "long hair" in Greek, i.e., long-haired star, and comets were often described as beautiful women with long hair. Medusa, who we will discuss in the next chapter, was one such Greek mythological figure described as a once beautiful woman with long, beautiful hair until she was transformed into a monster and her hair transformed into serpents. Like the Cosmic Crocodile, she was also decapitated. Thus Samson's haircut would be the mythological equivalent to the decapitations of the Cosmic Crocodile, Rahu and Medusa.

Like the Mayan Bacabs who neglected their duty to hold up the sky, Samson likewise caused the sky, i.e. the temple roof, to fall onto the Philistines. In an earlier episode Samson lit the tails of hundreds of foxes on fire, which caused a Philistine city to be consumed in fire, a likely reference to a meteor storm that preceded the main impact, i.e., temple collapse.

Curiously, Samson also used the jawbone of an ass to kill an entire Philistine army. In Mesoamerican myths, the Cosmic Crocodile, sometimes known as Cipactli, is frequently shown missing its lower jawbone. Likewise, the

Mexican deity of Tlaloc was often represented missing his lower jawbone and, like Medusa and Rahu, had large goggle eyes and enlarged, fang-like incisors.

One depiction of a Tlaloc headdress at the Mayan site of Yaxchilan showed him not only missing his lower jaw but also included a five-pointed star symbol as his eye with the long tail feathers of a Quetzal bird extending from his bodiless head. All of this symbolism seems strongly "cometary" and related to the Cosmic Crocodile myth.

Yaxchilan, Lintel 41, shows figure on right wearing Tlaloc headdress with star eye and long tail feathers of a Quetzal.

Also interesting is that the figure wearing the Tlaloc headdress is also wearing spotted regalia suggestive of a jaguar and thus of sunspots. Again, the symbolism seems consistent with the previous interpretation of a comet being decapitated by a solar flare or coronal mass ejection while the sun was covered in sunspots.

Like the four Bacabs that the Maya believed held up the sky, the Aztecs believed four Tlalocs held up the sky. Tlaloc was also associated with rains of fire reminiscent of

Samson's fire fox escapade. The exact meaning of the jawbone symbol is unknown but perhaps it represented a fragment that broke off of the main "head" of the comet.

Artwork of Tlaloc presiding over what most academics say is rain but actually appears to be a meteor shower. Note the many stars on his regalia.

In one part of the Biblical narrative, Samson battled a lion. Lions were often symbols of the sun thus this could represent Samson, a long-haired star (comet), being attacked by the Sun. This is reminiscent of the Aztec myth of the battle between Tezcatlipoca and Quetzalcoatl in which Quetzalcoatl (comet) battled a jaguar which resulted in Quetzalcoatl being hurled to Earth. The jaguar, a spotted cat, is a perfect symbol for the sun during an active period when it has sunspots thus this story likely encodes the effect of a solar flare or coronal mass ejection on a comet that caused it to fragment and impact the Earth.

There was another curious episode involving Samson's lion. After killing the lion Samson departed and then on his way back he passed the lion again. Bees had made a hive in the carcass of the lion and Samson ate some of their honey. Interestingly, Munya Andrews noted in her book *The Seven Sisters of the Pleiades* that the Pleiades have been associated with bees and honey in many cultures around the world[147]. This is because the star group rises again above the horizon in the middle of May, a time when flowers are in bloom and bees are active. Thus this reference to bees and honey in the Samson story could represent a mythological attempt to encode where in the sky these events took place: near the Pleiades asterism. As noted previously, the Pleiades are in the constellation Taurus and are associated with the yearly Taurid meteor shower which is made of debris from Comet Encke. A large meteor from the Taurid meteor stream is thought to have exploded over Tunguska in Russian Siberia and leveled over 800 square miles of forest.

Researchers have noted that the Mayan Bacabs were also associated with bees and honey. For instance, the story of the destruction of the world by a great flood is told on page 74 in the *Dreseden Codex*. The word *Bacab* is also referenced on this page but is spelled in a slightly unusual way. It is spelled as *bakabi* instead of *bakaba*. In Mayan, *kaabi* means "bee/honey/hive" thus associating the Bacabs with bees and honey[148] and also the Pleiades.

Finally, Samson's name meant "man of the Sun" which was likely an allusion to the brightness of the fireball that resulted as the comet fragment entered the atmosphere. This recalls the eyewitness account from Tunguska which noted the meteor was as bright as the sun.

Thus we see many of these myths in the Old World and the New World seem to encode a struggle or battle between a comet and the sun in which the final outcome was a breakup and devastating impact event on Earth.

19. Medusa: A Greek Account

The Greek account of Medusa sounds remarkably similar to the Mayan Flood Myth and its decapitation of a Cosmic Crocodile.

In Greek mythology, Medusa was a gorgon who once had long beautiful hair. Gorgons were always represented with large, wild eyes. According to Wikipedia,

> *"The large eyes, as well as Athena's "flashing" eyes, are symbols termed "the divine eyes"...appearing also in Athena's bird, the owl. They can be represented by spirals, wheels, concentric circles, swastikas, firewheels, and other images."*[149]

Thus we see Medusa was associated with spirals and swastikas just like Rahu, the Cosmic Crocodile, and Quetzalcoatl. Depictions of Medusa are nearly identical to those of Rahu. She had spirals in her hair and an open mouth with fangs identical to those of Rahu (see chapter 17).

Above: Archaic (Etruscan) fanged, goggle-eyed Gorgon. Compare with image of Rahu from chapter 17. (Courtesy Wikipedia. See color version on back cover.)

According to myth, Medusa's beautiful long hair was turned to serpents after she was raped by Poseidon, god of the sea. It should be noted that the word *comet* in Greek means "long-haired" since they saw comets as long-haired stars; thus, Medusa certainly had a comet association. Like the Cosmic Crocodile and Rahu, Medusa's head was also severed from her body. One version of the myth noted that Perseus, the doer of the deed, used a sword from Haephestus in order to accomplish this task. Curiously, Haephestus also created the chariot used by Helios, the sun god, thus it is clear that his creations were associated with the sun. Could this sword have represented a solar flare or coronal mass ejection like the Sudarshan Chakra used by Vishnu to sever Rahu's head from his body?

To accomplish this deed Perseus also borrowed the winged shoes of Hermes in order to fly across the sky. Here again Hermes is associated with a myth that appears to encode destruction brought by a comet as discussed in chapter 10, "Quetzalcoatl & Hermes: Cosmic Messengers."

Medusa was also associated with a flood and blood rain. According to myth, Perseus flew to Ethiopia where the sea god Poseidon had caused a massive flood and a sea monster, Cetus, had devoured a town. Curiously, in Greek art most cetea (plural of Cetus) are depicted as serpentine fish. In one version of the myth Perseus used Medusa's head to turn Cetus to stone. A serpent-like monster that was turned to stone and caused a sea flood that devoured a town is a perfect metaphor for a flaming meteor with long smoky tail slamming into the ocean causing a mega-tsunami and later witnesses discovering large rocks (meteor fragments) where the impact occurred.

Although in this instance the head of Medusa did not cause the flood, her previous rape by Poseidon, which turned her into the hideous monster with snakes in her hair, certainly linked her to the flood event. Medusa's head also dripped blood on the way to Ethiopia, a possible reference to blood rain or red rain that is similar to the "flood of blood" that resulted from the decapitation of the Cosmic Crocodile. Thus the story of Medusa has many of the same elements as the previous myths that appear to encode a comet fragmentation and impact event.

Since we now have a physical location for this flood and impact event, is there any physical evidence in these locations that would support our impact hypothesis? In fact, there is.

There is evidence of a mega-tsunami impacting the eastern shores of Africa around this time. Astronomer Dallas Abbott has argued that the chevron-shaped geological formations on the island of Madagascar were formed by an ancient mega-tsunami.[150] Each of these chevron-shaped formations are two-times larger than Manhattan. Each formation is over 600 feet high, taller than the Chrysler Building, suggesting the wave that deposited this debris was *at least* this tall but likely much taller.

Abbott believes the nearby Burckle Crater in the Indian Ocean was the location for this impact.[151] Abbott noted this crater was between 4000-5000 years old thus it could easily have formed around 3300 BC at the time recorded in the Mayan Flood Myth. This event would not only have impacted the coasts of eastern Africa but also India. This could explain why the legend of Medusa and Ramu are so similar.

These large chevron-shaped tsunami deposits may also explain another aspect of the Mayan Flood Myth. Throughout Mesoamerica, myths related that the body of the Cosmic Crocodile was used to form new Earth after the deluge. In fact, some depictions of this crocodile included chevrons on its back which were said to represent mountains. The fact that these impact-induced mega-tsunamis deposited such immense mountainous debris fields in the shape of chevrons is likely the origin of these associations between crocodiles and newly created land following a great flood.

Interestingly, depictions of Medusa are also strongly similar to the Aztec god Tlaltecuhtli, who famously appears in the center of the Aztec Calendar Stone. According to Wikipedia:

> *"In one of the Mexica creation accounts Tlaltecuhtli is described as a sea monster who dwelled in the ocean after the fourth Great Flood, an embodiment of the raging chaos before creation. Quetzalcoatl and Tezcatlipoca, in the form of serpents, tore [her]*

in half, throwing half upwards to create the sky and stars and leaving the other half to become the land of the earth."[152]

The similarities between the myth of Tlaltecuhtli and those of Rahu, Medusa and the Cosmic Crocodile are obvious. Again we have a story of a deity being torn in half with one part remaining in the heavens and one part coming to Earth from which new land was created. By placing the face of Tlaltecuhtli in the center of the Aztec Calendar Stone or Stone of the Fifth Sun it is suggestive that the Aztecs believed she would play some part in the end of the Fifth Sun, our current era.

Above: Tlaltecuhtli as seen in the center of the Aztec Calendar Stone (Courtesy Wikipedia. See color version on back cover.)

A large statue of Tlaltecuhtli was recently unearthed in Mexico which had even greater similarities to the previous Medusa/gorgon image. This Tlaltecuhtli had the curly or spiral hair of Medusa along with the outstretched tongue. A gorgon/Medusa image created in Syracuse, Sicily in the 5th century BC is eerily similar.

Above: Sculpture of Tlaltecuhtli showing the Medusa-like curly hair and extended tongue. (See color version on back cover.)

Gorgon from Syracuse, Sicily, 5th century BC with spiral hair, extended tongue, and fangs. Note the swastika-like configuration of arms and legs.

Rahu depicted with the same curly/spiral hair as Medusa and Tlaltecuhtli and the fangs, mustache-beard and earspools similar to Tlaloc. (Courtesy Wikipedia)

What can account for such strong similarities between how these mythological characters, Rahu, Medusa, Tlaloc and Tlatecuhtli, were portrayed across three separate continents? The similarities in the myths can be readily explained by the fact that these ancient peoples all witnessed the same event in the night sky and simply recorded what they saw. But there is no such explanation for why they would all choose to depict this character in identical ways. This strongly suggests there was contact between these cultures at some point in the distant past. The Greeks and Hindus could certainly have had contact that would explain the similarities in depictions of Ramu and Medusa. Yet what explains these same similarities in the depiction of Tlaltecuhtli and Tlaloc in Mexico?

As we will see in the next chapter there is one more culture that features a bodiless, fanged deity missing its lower jaw that first appeared around 3300 BC and may hold the key to unraveling the mystery. It is the country most closely associated with dragons: China.

20. Taotie: A Chinese Account

There is one final bodiless monster among the world's great cultures: the *taotie* of China. One researcher noted, "The 'monster' often lacks a lower jaw and usually displays wide eyes...."[153] It first appeared on bronze vessels during the Shang and Zhou dynasties. According to Wikipedia:

> *The Taotie...sometimes translated as a gluttonous ogre mask... is a motif commonly found on Chinese ritual bronze vessels from the Shang and Zhou Dynasty. The design typically consists of a zoomorphic mask...with a pair of raised eyes and typically no lower jaw area. Some argue that the design can be traced back to jade pieces found in Neolithic sites such as the Liangzhu culture (3310–2250 BCE.*[154]

Once again we see this "mythical" creature was depicted with goggle eyes and without a lower jaw and first appeared around 3310 BC, the exact time period recorded in the Mayan Flood Myth. The word *'taotie'* first appeared in an ancient Chinese text where it was used "to refer to one of the four evil creatures of the world."[155] A passage in the ancient Chinese text *Spring and Autumn Annals* noted, "*The taotie...has a head but no body. When it eats people, it does not swallow them, but harms them.*"

Again, like the Cosmic Crocodile, Medusa, and Khetu the *taotie* was seen as a decapitated head. In another ancient Chinese text the *taotie* was referred to as one of the nine children of the dragon and was a creature that liked water. This reveals that the *taotie* was associated with a comet (dragon) and oceanic impact event (water) which is identical to the previous "mythical" deities. Furthermore, the term *taotie* was associated with gluttony which likely stemmed from the fact that this impact event "consumed" untold lives.

Researchers have noted that this *taotie* is nearly identical to the Olmec dragon or 'were-jaguar.'[156] The Olmecs were the mother culture of all Mesoamerican cultures including the Maya and Aztecs. Researchers have long noted many similarities between the Olmecs and Shang dynasty China. The similarities are so extensive that some have argued that this could only have been the result of direct contact between the Shang dynasty and Mesoamerica.[157]

Liangzhu Jade Ritual Taotie (2000 B.C.) Courtesy Dr. Mike Xu

Olmec Jade Ritual Sharpener featuring Olmec dragon (900 - 600 B.C.) Courtesy Dr. Mike Xu

One important design element in both of the above figures is the cleft head. In Olmec mythology the cleft resulted from a rain of stone axe heads that occurred after the previously mentioned battle between Quetzalcoatl and Tezcatlipoca. As one scholar noted:

> *"a jaguar god who was...the forerunner of the important Aztec god Tezcatlipoca, [was] conceived of in one phase as a jaguar. 'Thunderbolts' or stone axes,'rained from heaven,' were attributed to his activities. Saville speculated that the cleft in the forehead characteristic of these jaguar axes was caused by the blow on the head received during his struggle with Quetzalcóatl, at which time he was transformed into a jaguar."*[158]

As noted previously, the battle between a sky serpent (Quetzalcoatl) and a jaguar or spotted-cat god (Tezcatlipoca) is consistent with the interpretation that a comet was fragmented by a coronal mass ejection hurled from the sun during a period of heightened solar activity when it was covered in spots. The fact that this myth also recorded that a rain of stone axes occurred afterwards is also consistent with this interpretation since the fragmentation event would have created an enormous amount of rocky debris that would have rained down upon Earth.

The Olmec dragon is also often depicted with "flame eyebrows" which is also consistent with this interpretation since this design motif perfectly symbolizes a meteor as it enters the atmosphere with its face on fire.

Additionally, on Olmec pottery known as "dragon bowls" that featured stylized versions of the Olmec dragon with flame eyebrows can also be found a swastika-like symbol which further connects this deity with the swastika-shaped comet.

Olmec dragon bowl with flame eyebrows and swirling, swastika-like design.

Thus every ancient "myth" appears to have preserved important details that when added together paint a clearer picture of this catastrophic impact event in 3300 BC.

It seems highly unlikely that both the Chinese and Olmecs independently came up with identical designs for their dragons down to the same cleft head. If these were the only similarities between the two cultures one might be able to dismiss them as coincidental. Yet scholars have found many more similarities between the Olmec and Shang dynasty China.

For instance, Olmec writing appears very similar to early Chinese writing during the Shang dynasty. In fact, a Chinese scholar familiar with ancient Chinese writing was able to translate inscriptions on an Olmec sculpture with no problem.[159]

Although no expert on either Olmec or Chinese writing, I too was able to make a connection between these two ancient writing systems. For instance, one Shang character looked exactly like our modern letter **T**. In Chinese this character was pronounced "Shi" and meant "spirit."[160]

In Mayan, a T-shaped glyph pronounced "Ik" also meant "life, spirit, breath, wind."[161] What are the odds that two separate cultures would use the same symbol to represent the same concept?

Mayan IK glyph meaning "breath, life, spirit"

      Furthermore, one researcher noted that the Mayan IK glyph was "found in structurally similar positions to the Maya quincunx glyph"[162] suggesting the two glyphs were closely related. The diamond-shaped quincunx glyph was also used for the Mayan word EK which meant "star" and was also used for the Mayan calendar day name LAMAT which meant "Venus." This same researcher found that "both the IK glyph and the quincunx could have meanings such as 'life, breath, wind' while participating in glyphic constructions meaning 'death';"[163] thus, we see that the quincunx glyph had associations with spirit, death and star.

Mayan quincunx glyph meaning "star, Venus"

Interestingly, a diamond-shaped symbol identical to the Mayan quincunx appeared on the forehead of the Chinese *taotie* monster. Did this symbol have the same meaning in China as in Mesoamerica: spirit, death and star? Is this why it was placed in the center of taotie's head? Curiously meteors or falling stars were seen by many cultures as the souls of the dead returning to Earth thus it would seem that a symbol associated with spirit, death and star would be appropriate on a design meant to represent a meteor that consumed innumerable lives.

This Shang dynasty taotie has a diamond-shaped design in the center of its head similar to the Mayan quincunx glyph.

More importantly, this researcher also noted that the Mayan glyph IK, "wind" was the name of a day on the Mayan calendar. The equivalent day on the Aztec calendar was named Ehecatl which also meant "wind." Ehecatl was also another name for Quetzalcoatl. Quetzalcoatl was, as noted in chapter 8, associated with Venus and the Lamat glyph was also associated with Venus. Clearly all of these symbols were closely related and centered around

Quetzalcoatl. Thus the *taotie* and Quetzalcoatl clearly represented the same comet fragmentation event.

Once again, if these were the only similarities they could be dismissed as coincidence but when added to the previously mentioned similarities the odds are against chance and in favor of some form of contact between ancient China and Mesoamerica. And as we will see in the next chapter it appears that even the Mayan calendar itself had a Chinese origin. But was it the Chinese or some other group who were responsible for these connections?

21. The Other Legend of Kukulkan & the True Origins of the Mayan Calendar

Curiously, there are legends around the world in far flung places such as China, Central America, South America and Easter Island that a race of tall, white-skinned, bearded, blonde and/or red-haired and blue-eyed foreigners re-established civilization after a great flood. In fact, the myth of Kukulkan/Quetzalcoatl was closely associated with this legend. This strong association between Quetzalcoatl and fair-skinned, bearded foreigners is part of the reason the Aztecs miscalculated the true intentions of the Spanish when they first arrived and allowed them to enter their capital city because they thought these strangers might be the prophesied return of Quetzalcoatl.

Always dismissed by mainstream academics as fanciful, evidence of such foreigners was actually unearthed in China in 1977. Archaeologists discovered the burials of obviously Caucasian people preserved in the sands of the Takla Makan desert in western China. Referred to as the Tarim mummies[164] as well as the Tocharians, these burials featured tall, bearded Caucasians with blonde and red hair and blue eyes.

One burial revealed a man with a tattoo on his face. The tattoo was in the shape of a spiral identical to those found associated with Quetzalcoatl in Mexico. He was also found with a helmet featuring a swastika design. As noted previously the swastika was the shape of the comet known by the Chinese as the "long-tailed pheasant star" and by Mesoamericans as Kukulkan/Quetzalcoatl. Thus this Tocharian man not only looked like the legendary Kukulkan but also was associated with the symbols of Kukulkan discussed previously: a spiral and swastika.

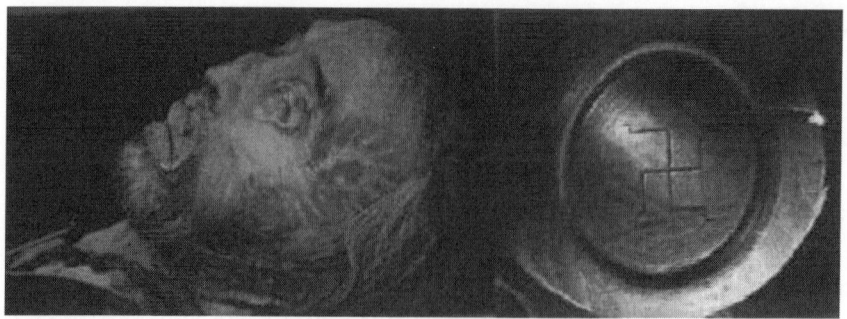

Spiral tattoo and swastika helmet of Caucasian Tarim mummy found in China.

Even more interesting is that both bronze artifacts and the wheel were found in Tocharian settlements that predated their earliest use in China. These settlements were all located along the Silk Road, the primary trade route into China from the west. This suggests the Tocharians were traders and likely responsible for bringing these important technologies to China, just as the legends claimed. As one researcher noted:

> *"The new finds are also forcing a reexamination of old Chinese books that describe historical or legendary figures of great height, with deep-set blue or green eyes, long noses, full beards, and red or blond hair. Scholars have traditionally scoffed at these accounts, but it now seems that they may be accurate."*[165]

Although the mummies discovered so far date to 1800 BC researchers dated the first arrival of the Tocharians in China to around 5,000 years ago circa 3000 BC. In other words, it appears they arrived in China soon after the 3300 BC event recorded in the Mayan Flood Myth.

Researchers noted that legends in Peru about Vira Cocha revealed that this tall, light-skinned, bearded, blue-eyed man also arrived during a time of darkness and was associated with a great flood after which he reestablished civilization by teaching the survivors metal working and agriculture.[166]

In Colombia and Panama the natives had a similar legend about a bearded leader named Bochica:

> *"...Bochica was a bearded man who came from the east. He taught the primitive Chibcha people ethical and moral norms and gave them a model by which to organize their states, with one spiritual and one secular leader. Bochica also taught the people agriculture, metalworking and other crafts before leaving for the west."*[167]

The legends go on to recount how their civilization was eventually destroyed by a flood and Bochica returned to help them.

The South American legends noted that these red-haired foreigners departed to the west thus it should come as no surprise that west of Peru on isolated Easter Island comes the next legends of red-headed foreigners bringing the building blocks of civilization. Yet this time there are eyewitness accounts by early explorers of these white, red-haired foreigners to corroborate the legends.

As one researcher noted:

> *When European explorers first discovered Easter Island and Tahiti, there were many reports of white people with red hair amongst the native population. For example Mendana, who sailed through the Pacific in 1595, visited an island in the Tuamotus and reported that the chief had "a mass of red and rather curly hair, reaching half way down his back." Captain Roggveen's visit to Easter Island in 1722, recorded that amongst the first natives to come aboard their ship was the chief who was "an entirely white man." All the early visitors to Easter Island*

noted that some of the islanders were not only very fair and tall, but had soft, reddish hair, with greenish, blue eyes. On many islands in southern Polynesia, these people were often found to be holding positions of high rank, but as the years went by, less and less sightings were reported. From the early accounts by Captain Wallis, who voyaged to Tahiti twice, noted that the paler red heads in Tahiti were succumbing to disease brought by European ships more readily than the black haired people. This one fact alone indicates that the ancestry of Pacific Caucasians was not from Europe.[168]

Easter Island is most famous for the enormous stone heads often topped with a red stone called a *pukao* meant to represent the top-knot of hair of these red-haired people.

The first known painting of Easter Island in 1775 by William Hodges. Note the red stones called 'pukao' placed on top.

Geologist Robert Schoch has made a connection between these stone heads of Easter Island and the Gobekli Tepe site in Turkey mentioned in chapter 4, the oldest temple site in the world dating back to 10,000 BC. He noted:

> "Both the moai and the anthropomorphic central pillars of Enclosure D at Gobekli Tepe have arms and hands positioned similarly against the body, with hands and fingers extended over the belly and navel region."[169]

These same types of statues with this same configuration of hands and fingers over the belly can also be found in Peru where these red-haired foreigners are said to have originally lived before arriving on Easter Island. Could the Gobekli Tepe site represent one of the earliest sites of the Tocharians? Could Easter Island represent one of their final outposts thousands of years later on one of the most isolated islands on Earth?

More importantly, the legends surrounding Quetzalcoatl/Kukulkan in Mexico also state that he was a fair-skinned, bearded man who brought civilization to Mexico. Could this legend refer to the Tocharians? Could these be the people whom the Aztecs mistook the Spanish for?

As noted in the previous chapter, many researchers over the years have noted similarities between Chinese culture and Mesoamerican culture. Yet one scholar, David B. Kelley, has even noted similarities between the Chinese calendar and the calendars used throughout Mesoamerica. For instance, both cultures used calendars with similar names for the days. Not only were the day names similar and, in some instances, identical but their order in the calendars was also the same in both cultures.

For example, the Chinese calendar day name, "dragon," was the first day of their calendar. The first day in the Mayan calendar was named *Imix* which means "crocodile" and in the Aztec calendar was named *Cipactli* which means "crocodile." As was noted previously the Mayan Cosmic Crocodile and the Aztec Cipactli both seem to refer to the comet discussed in the Mayan Flood Myth. Likewise it has been argued that dragons were also a way to symbolize comets. Interestingly, in Chinese belief dragons were also associated with water. Thus we see that the Mayan crocodile and Aztec Cipactli were Mesoamerican versions of the Chinese dragon and all three cultures used this creature as the name for the first day of their respective calendars.[170] This is just one example. Kelley noted many more and concluded:

> *"there is a systematic relationship between the Chinese, Aztec, and Maya elements"* and that *"there appears to be enough similarity in the Chinese and Mesoamerican data to come to the conclusion that it is improbable that coincidence is the primary cause."*[171]

This is just one of many, many examples of similarities between Chinese culture and Mesoamerican cultures that have led some researchers to theorize that there was contact between these two cultures. But could there be another option? Could these Tocharians be the very people who influenced *both* cultures, the Chinese *and* the Mesoamericans, and this explains the similarities as opposed to direct contact from China to Mexico? Did both cultures receive the same teachings from these foreigners but simply filtered them through their own cultural machinery that resulted in some aspects being emphasized in one culture while being ignored in the other; thus each culture developed similarly, but independently, from the seed planted by foreigners?

The fact that both cultures have legends of tall, blonde and red-haired, blue-eyed foreigners bringing the building blocks of civilization (including their respective calendars) it seems a real possibility that this is the case. Mesoamerican scholars, like their Chinese counterparts, dismiss the legends surrounding Quetzalcoatl/Kukulkan as fanciful nonsense.

Yet there is now physical evidence to support the Chinese legends of foreign culture bearers. So why should we doubt the Mesoamerican legends which were identical to the Chinese legends?

Curiously, geneticists have discovered that the gene for blue eyes only appeared between 6,000 and 10,000 years ago.[172] Could the genetic mutation that created the blue eyes of the Tocharians have been a direct result of increased radiation from the Sun or increased cosmic radiation from the Galactic Center that occurred at the time of the super solar storm or galactic superwave in 10,500 BC discussed in chapters 12 and 13? Are they the ones who gave the Maya information about a green sky serpent, Kukulkan-Quetzalcoatl, that appeared in 10,500 BC around the time of this great catastrophe and would return in 2004 as a sign of a new age of disasters? Is this why the legend of Kukulkan/Quetzalcoatl was associated with both a green sky serpent and a race of fair-skinned, bearded people who brought civilization to Mexico?

The dating of the previously discussed Gobekli Tepe fits within this time period and begs the question: was it created by the Tocharians who eventually moved into western China by 3000 BC after the comet catastrophe of 3300 BC? Is this the reason the sculptures at Gobekli Tepe and Easter Island have similar designs despite being separated by thousands of years?

If true then it seems that after the catastrophic events of 3300 BC one of the few, or only, advanced stone age civilizations that survived sent out exploratory missions to see who remained. They discovered that most of the coastal civilizations around the world had been destroyed and so they taught the survivors the basics of how to rebuild a civilization from scratch. The legends say these foreigners taught the locals art, architecture, mathematics, government, and more — all the requisites of civilized life.

Is this why civilizations all over the world appeared to have emerged around 3200 BC? Have our scientists been mistaken in their belief that this was the *emergence* of civilization but instead was really the *re-emergence* of civilization? Did survivors of this catastrophe simply move inland and reestablished their civilizations in safer locales? Did the Tocharians help in this process and, more importantly, provided them with calendars that encoded the arrival time of the next cosmic catastrophe?

Is this cosmic catastrophe the very event the Mayan calendar was designed to encode? What, *exactly*, did the Maya believe would happen at the end of the current calendar cycle?

VI. The 2012 Prophecy

21. Decoding the Aztec Calendar Stone

The Aztec Calendar Stone was carved in 1427. The artisans included a wealth of information encoded on this stone about the Aztec belief in a cycle of cosmic destructions that had befallen Earth four times in the past. They believed we currently lived in the fifth such era or Fifth Sun and that this age would also be destroyed.

At the top of the Aztec Calendar Stone was the date 13 Reed, the date the Aztecs believed the Fourth Sun was destroyed by flood and the Fifth Sun was born. The date 13 Reed corresponded with the year 1011 AD in our Gregorian calendar.

In 1980, astronomer Anthony Aveni noted in his book *Skywatchers of Ancient Mexico* that there appeared to be star patterns or constellations carved into the flanges (i.e., the rock edges) of the Aztec Calendar Stone. In 1999 astronomer Robert S. McIvor published a paper in the *Journal of the Royal Astronomical Society of Canada* entitled "Star Patterns on the Aztec Calendar Stone" in which he hypothesized that one of these star patterns represented the Milk Ladle asterism (star group) located within the constellation Sagittarius and another represented three prominent stars in the constellation Aquila, the Eagle.

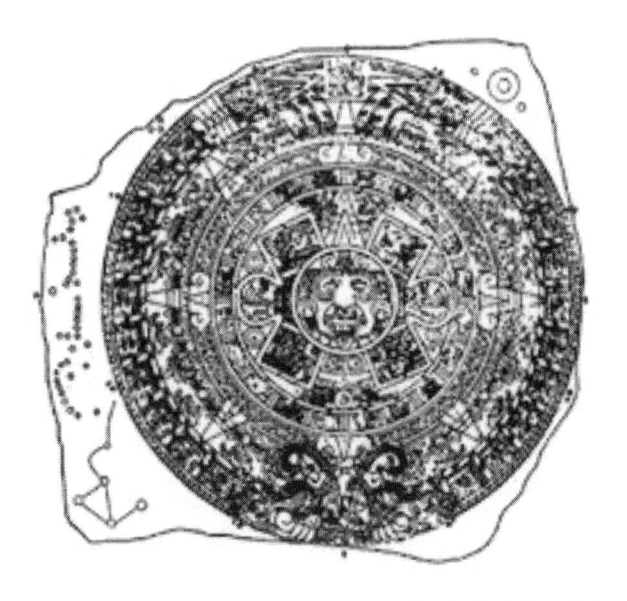

Notice the constellations carved on the left side of the Aztec Calendar Stone.

McIvor also noted that according to Chinese records, a "guest star" appeared near the Milk Ladle asterism (known to them as the asterism Nan-tou or the Rice Ladle) in 1011 AD. In Chinese astronomy a "guest star" represented any light in the night sky that appeared and disappeared over a short period of time such as a comet or super nova. McIvor theorized that the carving of both the 1011 AD date and the Milk Ladle asterism on the Aztec Calendar Stone possibly were connected to this Chinese "guest star" event.

What message did the Aztecs intend to send by encoding all of this information (the date 1011 AD, the Milk Ladle asterism from the Sagittarius constellation, and three stars from the Aquila constellation) on the Aztec Calendar Stone? And what type of "guest star" did the Chinese spot near the Milk Ladle in 1011 AD: a comet, super nova or something else entirely?

In 1997, physicist Paul A. LaViolette wrote a book entitled *Earth Under Fire*. In this book he theorized that the intense radio source at the direct center of our galaxy, Sagittarius A, was a star not a black hole and periodically it had enormous outbursts of energy and matter called a galactic superwave. We know such outbursts occur at the centers of other galaxies. Coincidentally, Sagittarius A and the center of the Galaxy appear in our night sky near the Milk Ladle asterism in the constellation Sagittarius.

(Credit: ESA/NASA/AVO/Paolo Padovani. See color version on front cover.)

LaViolette theorized that these outbursts from Sagittarius A would be devastating to life on earth. In fact, the last such large outburst appears to coincide with the onset of the Younger Dryas climate event in 10,500 BC and the great mass extinction which accompanied it which included the demise of mastadons, wooly mammoths, saber toothed tigers and more. He theorized that a smaller outburst occurred around 3300 BC which coincided with the date recorded in the Mayan Flood Myth.

LaViolette theorized that when Sagittarius A, which is not visible to the naked eye, experienced one of these outbursts it would appear to persons on earth as the sudden appearance of a new bright blue star. This "guest star" would then fade from view once the eruption was over yet the energy and mass it erupted would be hurling through space directly towards Earth.

Does the Chinese guest star of 1011 AD near Nan-tou, the Milk Ladle asterism, represent such an eruption of Sagittarius A? If so, what effects did it have on Earth? The Aztecs claimed the Fourth Sun, which ended in 1011 AD, was destroyed by a flood. Is there any evidence of such a flood? In fact, there is.

The *Anglo-Saxon Chronicle* states that in England 1014 AD, on the eve of St. Michael's day (September 28, 1014),

> *"came the great sea-flood, which spread wide over this land, and ran so far up as it never did before, overwhelming many towns, and an innumerable multitude of people."*[173]

This is clearly a reference to a tsunami similar to the one that struck Indonesia in December 2004 and killed over 250,000 people.

What could have caused this tsunami? Unlike the Pacific Ocean, the Atlantic Ocean is not known for earthquakes since it is located on a tectonic plate boundary that is spreading apart along the Mid Atlantic Ridge not colliding with another plate. Thus what else could be responsible for the flood recorded in the Anglo-Saxon Chronicle? Could a meteor or comet impact in the Atlantic Ocean have been the cause?

Researcher Dallas Abbott of the Lamont Doherty Earth Observatory at Columbia University discovered material in a bog at Black Rock Forest in Cornwall, New York that "is difficult to explain except with an impact event." This material included impact glass and spherules that can only be created by the forces associated with a meteor or comet impact as well as marine sediments and fossils that were determined to have come from the mid-Atlantic ridge, over 3800 kilometers from Black Rock Forest. Abbott noted, "because these locations are so far away from Black Rock Forest, the only viable method for transporting the material to Black Rock Forest is an impact event."[174]

In other words, the evidence suggests that a comet or meteor slammed into the middle of the Atlantic Ocean and ejected material from the bottom of the ocean, which flew over 3800 kilometers and landed in the bog at Black Rock Forest in New York. The material at Black Rock was dated to around 1014 AD. Abbott also noted that such an impact event would have also created a tsunami that would have radiated out in all directions from the point of impact thus she began looking for evidence of such a tsunami.

In addition to the afore-mentioned tsunami in England on September 28, 1014, researchers in North Carolina noted that either a major storm surge or tsunami devastated the coastal areas of the state around this time as well.[175] The wave wiped the Outer Banks off the map and it took four hundred years for them to reform. Considering all the evidence for a major Atlantic tsunami at this time it was most likely this tsunami not storm surge that devastated coastal North Carolina.[176]

Abbott also found tsunami deposits in the Lesser Antilles in the Caribbean that also dated to around 1014 AD. By noting the angle of the tsunami deposits in both England and the Lesser Antilles, Abbott was able to deduce the probable location of the impact in the middle of the Atlantic Ocean. All of this evidence showed that the tsunami impacted the coastlines on both sides of the Atlantic and thus affected millions of people living along those coasts.

Abbott also noted there was a "prominent ammonium anomaly," i.e., an increase in ammonia in the atmosphere, as represented in Antarctic ice core data associated with the year 1014 AD. This same spike in atmospheric ammonia can be seen associated with two other known impact events: the Tunguska, Russia event on June 30, 1908 and the Brazilian Tunguska of August 13, 1930. This provided more supporting evidence for an impact event in 1014 AD.

Other researchers going back through the historical record found that the 11th century featured some of the most active Taurid meteor showers ever recorded. I. S. Astapovich and A. K. Terent'eva conducted a study of fireballs appearing between the 1st and 15th centuries and revealed the Taurids to have been "the most powerful shower of the year in the 11th century (with 42 fireballs belonging to them) and no shower, not even the great ones, could be compared with them as to activity."[177] Thus the Taurid meteor storm of 1014 must have been truly an awe-inspiring spectacle even greater than the Leonid meteor storm of 1833.

Above: Leonid meteor storm of 1833 as seen at Niagara Falls, New York. (See color version on back cover.)

Thus all the evidence supports the theory that a meteor slammed into the middle of the Atlantic and produced tsunamis that impacted coasts on both sides of this ocean in the fall of 1014 AD.

Coincidentally, according to Aztec legend, their Fourth Sun ended in 1011 AD due to a great flood followed by the sky falling. This event is recorded on the Aztec Calendar Stone or Stone of the Fifth Sun that included two *xihucoatls*, "fire serpents," around the outside edge of the sculpture. Each "fire serpent" had a snout with seven star symbols that represented the seven stars of the Pleiades.[178] This suggests these "fire serpents" were flaming meteors emanating from the Pleiades and thus were part of the Taurid meteor stream. The Taurids are known for slow-moving fireballs with long smoke trails thus the designation of "fire serpent" is quite appropriate. The fact that the Fourth Sun ended with a flood is consistent with these "fire serpents" having impacted the ocean creating a tsunami. Yet their date of 1011 AD is two years off from the known impact date of 1014 AD. Why?

Researchers have noted that after the Aztecs won their independence in 1428 they revised many historical events to fall on important dates within their 52 year calendar cycle called the *xiuhmolpilli*.[179] One researcher noted, "A number of events of early history were assigned to dates with important positions in the 52-year cycle and that certain types of events were recorded as occurring in years of the same name."[180] Additionally, astronomer Anthony Aveni noted that "calendrical adjustments were frequently geared to the 52-year *xiuhmolpilli* or one [of] its multiples...."[181] Thus this could explain why the flood that ended the Aztec's Fourth Sun and resulted in the creation of the Fifth Sun is said to have taken place in 13 Reed, 1011 AD, instead of the actual date of 1014 AD.

The Taurids are active from early October until late November in modern times and a thousand years ago would have ranged from late September until mid November. Thus the date recorded in the *Anglo-Saxon Chronicle*, September 28, 1014 (October 4, 1014 AD in our modern Gregorian calendar), is consistent with an interpretation that two large meteors (fire serpents) part of the Taurid meteor stream crashed into the middle of the Atlantic Ocean and caused tsunamis that spread out and impacted shores all around its perimeter.

The Aztec Calendar Stone was associated with the New Fire Ceremony and this ceremony, in turn, was associated with the Pleiades. The New Fire Ceremony was conducted every 52 years when the Aztec's two primary calendars came back into sync. They called this event the "binding of years" and the New Fire ceremony marked the occasion.

The last New Fire ceremony took place in 1507 at the temple of *Huixachtlan* on the top of *Huixachtecatl*, "Hill of the Star." The "star" in question was the Pleiades asterism. According to the Franciscan missionary Bernardino de Sahagun who wrote a 12 volume history of Mexico the New Fire ceremony went something like this:

> ...they considered it a matter of belief that the world would come to an end at the conclusion of one of these bundles of years. They had a prophecy or oracle that at that time the movement of the heavens would cease, and they took as a sign [of this] the movement of the Pleiades. On the night of this feast, which they called Toximmolpilia [the Binding of the Years***] it so befell that the Pleiades were at the zenith at midnight with respect to the horizon in Mexico. On this night they made new fire, and before they made it, they extinguished all the fires in all the provinces, towns and houses in all of this

New Spain. And they went in a solemn procession. All of the priests and servants of the temple departed from here, the Temple of Mexico, during the first quarter of the night, and went to the summit of that mountain near Itztpalapan which they call Uixachtecatl. They reached the summit at midnight, or almost, where stood a great pyramid built for that ceremony. Having reached there, they looked at the Pleiades to see if they were at the zenith, and if they were not, they waited until they were. And when they saw that now they passed the zenith, they knew the movement of the heavens had not ceased, and that the end of the world was not then. [Vol. 4, p143]

And when they drew the new fire, they drew it there at Uixachtlan, at midnight, when the night divided in half, They drew it upon the breast of a captive, and it was a well-born one on whose breast [the priest] bored the fire drill. And when a little [fire] fell, when it took flame, then speedily [the priest] slashed open the breast of the captive, seized his heart, and quickly cast it there into the fire. [Vol. 7, p25]

Then [the priests] slashed open [the captive's] breast. In his breast [cavity] the new fire was drawn. They opened the breast of the captive with a flint knife called ixcuauac. [Vol. 7, p28]

These New Fire rituals were dedicated to the god *Huitzilopochtli*.[182] Curiously he was associated with birds and birds were given to him as offerings, primarily hawks and quail. (This recalls the bird cemeteries associated with Thoth mentioned in chapter 13.) Other ceremonies dedicated to this god also appear to reenact a meteor impact event. In fact, they seem reminiscent of the Chinese dragon dance. For instance, Sahagun's description of the annual *Panquetzalitztli* festivals, held in honor of *Huitzlilopochtli*, notes:

> *"in a concluding episode of the ritual events, a large paper-and-feather xihucoatl [fire serpent] was brought down the steps from the platform of the Main Pyramid, to be presented at an altar on the bottom landing: Thereupon likewise descended the fire serpent, looking like a blazing pine firebrand. Its tongue was made of red arara feathers, looking like a flaming torch. And its tail was of paper, two or three fathoms long. As it descended, it came moving its tongue, like that of a real serpent, darting in and out. And when [the priest] had come [with it], bringing it down to the base [of the pyramid], he proceeded carefully to the eagle vessel. Then he went up [to the eagle vessel] and raised [the fire serpent] also to the four directions. When he had [so] raised it up, then he cast it upon the sacrificial paper, and then they burned. (Sahagun 1951-70, Bk. 2:136)."*[183]

Aztec Eagle Vessel from Templo Mayor in Mexico City into which the flaming fire serpent was tossed (Courtesy Wikipedia)

A fire serpent descending from the heavens (i.e., top of the pyramid) and bursting into flames once reaching earth is the perfect metaphor for a meteor impact.

The date of the 1014 AD tsunami, falling on the eve of St. Michael's Day, is also interesting. The legends surrounding the Biblical character of Michael sound very reminiscent of an impact event:

> "there was war in heaven. Michael and his angels fought against the dragon, and the dragon and his angels fought back. But he was not strong enough, and they lost their place in heaven. The great dragon was hurled down - that ancient serpent called the devil, or Satan, who leads the whole world astray. He was hurled to the earth, and his angels with him."

As noted previously, comets were associated with serpents and dragons throughout the ancient world. This "war in heaven," then, sounds a lot like an eyewitness account of a comet fragmentation and impact event. The "dragon" would represent the parent comet and "his angels" were fragments of the comet as it broke apart. The dragon being "hurled down" and "hurled to the earth" would represent the impact event.

Yet this passage from the book of Revelation was written over 2,000 years ago, a thousand years before the impact event of 1014 AD. So why was September 28 already associated with Michael? This suggests that Earth has experienced a previous cosmic impact on September 28 during a previous era that was the basis of the story in Revelation and the reason the date was devoted to Michael, the hero of the impact allegory. Thus could there be a predictable cycle of such impacts? Instead of viewing the ancient writings as prophecies could they be closer to forecasts based on a predictable cycle?

Not only does the end of the Aztec's Fourth Sun correspond with a suspected impact event so does the end of their Third Sun. For instance, Aztec legends noted that the Third Sun ended with a rain of fire. They also noted that the beginning of the Fourth Sun was associated with the goddess *Chalchiuhtlicue* crying blood for 52 years producing destructive floods. Rains of fire, blood rain and floods are all known phenomenon associated with impact events.

Interestingly, these legends correspond well with events that happened on Earth beginning in the year 536 AD. Researchers have noted that Earth appears to have entered a dense cloud of cosmic dust that blocked out the sun for 18 months. Written records from the time noted how the sun only shown for four hours a day and was only as bright as the Sun during an eclipse. Other written records noted that real blood fell from the sky during this time followed by deadly plagues and that these events lasted for 52 years.

Researchers have discovered an ammonium spike in the ice core record dated to around 540 AD. As noted previously, these ammonium spikes are associated with known impact events thus there appears to have been such an impact event in 540 AD. Dallas Abott noted that evidence for at least two major tsunamis dated to this time period as well. Red rain or blood rain is also a known phenomenon associated with impact events thus eyewitness accounts of blood falling from the sky further supports this impact hypothesis. Thus the Aztec "myths" regarding the events associated with the end of the Third Sun, start of the Fourth Sun, and end of the Fourth Sun are consistent with actual events in 540 AD and 1014 AD.

Researchers have noted that another significant impact tsunami occurred around 1491 near Australia. Taking into account the 540 AD event, 1014 AD event and the 1491 AD event it thus appears that significant impact events occur every five hundred years that are capable of causing major regional destruction and global climatic disruptions.

    Astronomers have argued that not only is there a 500-year cycle but also a 3,000 year cycle of impact events associated with the Taurid meteor stream. This begs the question: did the Maya know of another cycle of cosmic catastrophes that occurred every 5,000 years for which their calendar cycle was designed to encode? Did they expect another impact on or around December 21, 2012?

22. Decoding Tortuguero's Monument 6

As we have seen so far, the Maya appeared to have recorded the actual date of a real event that devastated the ancient world 5,000 years ago. The event was undoubtedly the breakup of a comet and impact of its fragments into the Earth's oceans that led to immense mega-tsunamis that devastated coastal civilizations around the world. In one text the Maya referred to this comet as a Cosmic Crocodile or Crocodile Star. In another they referred to it as a Celestial Bird.

The Maya recorded that this event occurred near the end of the last calendar cycle. What did the Maya expect would happen the next time the calendar cycled ended? Did they also expect another devastating impact event?

The end of the Mayan 13th *Baktun* occurs on December 21, 2012. They recorded this date as 13.0.0.0.0, *4 Ahaw 3 Kankin*. One researcher noted that the date recorded on the previously discussed Mayan Blowgunner Vase was *1 Ahaw 3 Kankin* and thus "echoed the 2012 date."[184] As noted in chapter 17, this vase was likely also a record of the impact event that occurred near the end of the last Mayan calendar cycle. By echoing the end of the current calendar cycle, were the Maya suggesting they thought an impact event would be associated with the end of the current calendar cycle?

To explore this idea further we must turn to Monument 6 at the Tortuguero site in Tabasco, Mexico. This is the only Mayan "prophecy" that explicitly alludes to December 21, 2012. According to various interpretations, the inscription on Monument 6 notes that the deity *Bolon Yokte Kuh* will "descend" on 12/21/2012.

It has been noted that *Bolon Yokte* played an important part in the events at the end of the previous Mayan calendar cycle. In fact, one researcher noted he is related to the Avian Bird Deity[185], another name for the Celestial Bird. Thus the fact that the Tortuguero Monument 6 records that *Bolon Yokte*, the Celestial Bird, descends on December 21, 2012 is eerily similar to the impact event recorded on the Mayan Blowgunner Vase. Does this suggest that the Maya believed an impact event would occur on this date?

Researchers have noted that *Bolon Yokte Kuh* was both a "god of war and transition, and as such, he apparently attacks and destroys the supports which hold up the sky."[186] A deity that causes the sky to fall is also consistent with an interpretation that this deity is associated with an impact event. The fact that this text mentions the encircling of this deity while wearing robes is also interesting. As noted in chapter 8, "Comet Machholz and the Return of Kukulkan," comets were often described as wearing robes and, of course, comets' orbits could be described as "encircling"; thus, these parts of the prophecy are also consistent with an impact interpretation.

Researches have also noted that *Bolon Yokte* presided over *Katun 11 Ahau* in the *Katun* prophecies in the books of *Chilam Balam*. *Katun 11 Ahau* is always the first katun of a new cycle and served as a transition from *Katun 13 Ahau*, the final *katun* of the cycle. The next Katun 11 Ahau begins in 2052. As noted in chapter 6, "Predictions for Katun 13 Ahau (2032-2052)," the Mayan predictions for this time period sound remarkably like an impact event and NASA is currently tracking three asteroids which have a chance of hitting Earth during that time period. Thus *Bolon Yokte* serving as a transition between *Katun 13 Ahau* and *Katun 11 Ahau* is fitting if the Maya were trying to encode an impact event.

One final association of *Bolon Yokte* is also interesting. One researcher noted that *Bolon Yokte* appears to be associated with or one-in-the-same as God L.[187] Mayan depictions of God L always show him smoking a cigar. Researchers recorded an interesting prophecy in the Yucatan about a cigar-smoking god:

"THE CIGAR OF THE LORD OF HEAVEN

Have you seen the smoking stars (meteors) in the sky? Do you know what those things are? I am going to tell you what the smoking stars are.

The lord of the heaven daily smokes his cigar, the whole day he smokes his cigar. He is watching what the people here on earth are doing while he smokes his cigar. Because there are many bad people here on earth there are days when he get angry with us. He thinks then, "I am going to finish the life there on earth." He throws then his cigar butt, he flicks it with his finger.

Only because the beautiful lady virgin Mary feels sorry for us, she saves us. When she sees the lord of heaven has just thrown his cigar she quickly moves her hand. With the back of her hand she flicks the cigar butt into the sea. But the day is going to arrive when the beautiful lady virgin Mary will be fed up with us, she will then let the cigar fall here in the middle of the earth. On that day then the whole surface of the earth has to burn. Thus then all the people here on earth will die."[188]

If one needs an explicit reference to an impact event in order to accept the connection between *Bolon Yokte Kuh* with such events, one could do no better than this story.

Researchers have also noted that Tutuguero's Monument 6 is one of only two monuments that feature "deep-future forecasts,"[189] the other being the West Tablet from Palenque. Coincidentally, the West Tablet contains a "prophecy" that is also likely a reference to a future impact event.

Palenque was ruled by a man named Pakal who was born in 603 AD, just 63 years after the impact event of 540 AD. Pakal ruled Palenque for 68 years until his death in 683 AD. On the West Tablet from Palenque, a "prophecy" connects Pakal's accession date to a date in the far future: October 23, 4772.

Curiously, astronomers have noted that comet Swift-Tuttle has a small chance of collision with Earth on September 15, 4479[190]. Since the comet has a 133-year orbit even if it does not collide with Earth in 4479, its close approach could alter its orbit causing it to collide in one of its subsequent returns either in 4612 or 4745.

Swift-Tuttle is significantly larger than the asteroid that wiped out the dinosaurs thus an impact with this comet would be devastating to life on Earth. This would truly be the end of the world as we know it. Could the Maya have projected its orbit into the future and calculated a future impact around 4772? The astronomical and mathematical accomplishments of the Maya prove they were more than capable of making such forecasts.

Interestingly, the lid of Pakal's sarcophagus features a world tree with a Celestial Quetzal Bird at the top. The symbolism is quite similar to stela 2 from Izapa and the Mayan Blowgunner Vase both of which seem to be related to impact events. Was Pakal trying to send a message to the future about this deadly comet?

Above: Lid of Pakal's sarcophagus featuring a Celestial Bird at the top of a cross or World Tree. (Courtesy Wikipedia.)

Interestingly, the Mayan calendar's start date was August 11, 3114 BC. August 11th just happens to correspond to the peak night of the Perseid meteor shower. The Perseids are created by dust and debris from the Comet Swift-Tuttle. Did the Maya purposefully restart their calendar on this date to encode this meteor shower in order to alert the future about the dangers of Comet Swift-Tuttle?

Or was the calendar's start date incidental and, instead, it was purposefully designed to end on December 21, 2012 in order to coincide with a galactic alignment as theorized by John Major Jenkins in his book *Maya Cosmogenesis 2012*? As we have seen throughout this book the Galactic Center appears to have played a primary role in the events of both 10,500 BC and 3300 BC. Were the Maya purposefully using the end date of their calendar to direct our attention to the Galactic Center to highlight the dangers that lurk there?

23. End of the Cycle

As the preceding chapters have shown, a major impact event occurred near the end of the last calendar cycle and prophecies suggest another such event is expected around the end of the current calendar cycle. But the key word is "near." In fact, the impact event around 3300 BC occurred nearly two hundred years *before* the end of the previous calendar cycle that ended on August 11, 3114 BC.

The best way to think of this is to compare Mayan predictions to modern scientific forecasts. For instance, imagine a geologist who plotted on a linear timeline the date of every eruption of a particular volcano. After looking through his data suppose the geologist noted that the volcano appeared to erupt once every 5,000 years. Now imagine he realized that the last eruption was 4999 years ago. Would this mean that the volcano would erupt the next year on the very last day of the 5000-year cycle?

Of course not. That is not how cycles work. The volcano could erupt a week later, a month later or five years later. It could erupt twenty years later. Or it could have moved off its hotspot and never erupt again. The cycle only shows the average time between eruptions in the past. But once you reach the end of a cycle it lets you know that you have left the "safe zone" and that the probability of an eruption increases.

This is likely the same message the ancient Maya were trying to send to their future descendants by encoding this 5,000-year cycle into their calendar. They were likely trying to warn their descendants that at the end of the current calendar cycle the probability of a catastrophic impact event would increase.

But the fact is, we do not really understand why the Maya encoded a 5000-year cycle into their calendar. What we do know is that astronomers have determined that there appears to be a 300- year cycle, 500-year cycle, 1000-year cycle, and a 3,000-year cycle of impact events on Earth. Did the Maya know of a 5,000-year cycle that our scientists have yet to discover?

Based on the research for this book I believe this is very likely the case. It has become very clear over the course of researching and writing this book that all the Mesoamerican cultures from the Maya to the Aztecs believed in cycles of catastrophes that impacted Earth. Most of these catastrophes appear to have been impact events and the associated mega-tsunamis, floods, rains of fire, and dust-induced darkness and climate downturns associated with such events.

All Mesoamerican religion appears to have been focused on avoiding such catastrophes in the future through various rituals including human sacrifice. Is it a coincidence that riots broke out in the elite quarters of Teotihuacan after the impact event of 540 AD? Undoubtedly the elites and priests of this culture assured their citizens that they could protect them from future catastrophes. The citizens made their offerings, put up with the horror of human sacrifice, even offering up their own children for this purpose, yet despite all of these efforts and the assurances of their leaders, still another such event occurred. Would it not be easy to then turn on those same rulers who had now been exposed as the frauds they truly were?

The closest thing we have to compare this mindset to are the promises made to us by our elected officials after the tragedy of 9/11. Citizens were promised by their governments that no such terrorist act would ever be allowed to happen again. Citizens have given up many freedoms, sacrificed their children in wars, and subjected themselves to all manner of security "rituals" at airports and other locations all for the assurance that these things are necessary in order to prevent a future catastrophe like 9/11. We will take off our shoes, submit to body scans, pat downs, and strip searches and even allow our children to be subjected to the same all for the sake of preventing another such catastrophe.

Yet imagine what would happen if terrorists were able to board aircraft and duplicate the events of 9/11? This would prove that all of our sacrifices were in vain and all of the security "rituals" were nothing more than theatrics to make us *feel* safer without actually making us safer. Would we as citizens continue to believe our elected officials' guarantees that they could protect us? Or would we lose faith and even riot against our officials for their failures?

Once one understands the core fear underlying Mesoamerican beliefs, these cultures stop seeming so alien and become more human. They become just like us. They become people simply trying to make it day-to-day whose leaders preyed on their fears in order to enrich and empower themselves. With this knowledge, it is quite easy to relate to the ancient Maya despite all the superficial differences that previously made them seem so strange, foreign, and exotic.

The Maya were just like us except they knew a horrible truth about our past…and future. Our own astronomers and scientists are just beginning to learn this truth as well but there is still resistance to actually accepting that such catastrophes could happen to *us*, in our lifetimes. There is almost a sense of arrogance that somehow we are special and the laws of physics simply do not apply to us and our "advanced" civilization. Yet one can be assured, the laws of physics do not have exceptions for us. At some point our luck will run out and we, like our ancestors, will come face to face with the "stream from heaven," as Plato called it. And at that point the ancient "myths" will no longer seem so mythological and we will wish we had taken their warnings more seriously.

VII. The End

24. Conclusion

My research began with a simple question: why did many ancient Native American civilizations in the Southeastern United States only last for 250 years? This question eventually led me to discover the Mayan belief in a 256-year cycle that regulated the rise and fall of civilizations. From here I learned of the many prophecies or predictions the Maya had for the future and how accurate they had been for similar periods in the past.

I was shocked that in all the discussions in the mainstream media about the "end of the Mayan calendar" not once were the real Mayan prophecies ever discussed. Lots of conjecture and pontification about what the "end" of the Mayan calendar may or may not have meant; yet, nothing about the actual Mayan system of predictions based on repeating historic cycles. At this point I decided to dig deeper to learn what else the mainstream media, 2012 "true believers," and 2012 "debunkers" had missed in this discussion on the beliefs of the ancient Maya.

While doing further research I discovered that there was a 250-year seismic cycle, 250-year solar cycle and ~300 year impact cycle. In my attempt to understand the possible connections between these cycles I discovered that everything from disease outbreaks to insect infestations appeared to be influenced by solar cycles. More importantly, the human psyche appeared to be influenced both positively and negatively by these same solar cycles. Finally, my research led me to discover that another source of influence, namely the Galactic Center, was likely a contributing factor as well.

But what surprised me the most was how little we still knew about the universe. Things that ancient cultures seemed very aware of, i.e., periodic bombardments from the heavens leading to massive devastation on Earth, our "advanced" civilization only learned about in the past few decades. I was amazed at how accurate many of these Mayan "myths" were once one realized the reality of what they were describing. These "myths" stopped sounding superstitious and started sounding scientific.

Before undertaking this research I had no idea of the many dangers lurking in the Universe in which we live. I had no idea there were so many earth-crossing asteroids and comets. I had no idea that hidden dangers lurked within the beautiful meteor showers I watched in awe each year. I had no idea of the connection between the Galactic Center and life on earth. Who knew something so far away could have such serious consequences for life on Earth. Who knew the sun could possibly experience super-flares that could set forests on fire. Who knew meteors could cause mega-tsunamis that could wipe out entire civilizations with mountainous waves.

And who knew human beings could survive such unbelievable catastrophes? More amazing than the cosmic catastrophes was the awareness that all of us alive today had ancestors who witnessed these events, experienced these events and somehow managed to survive these events and passed the stories down to us.

This is what everyone in the 2012 debate has completely missed. It is not about whether the world will end or not. It is about *listening* to the stories of the past **not** *ignoring* them and making prudent decisions based on the lessons we can learn from them. It is inevitable that another super solar storm impacts Earth and we are simply not prepared for it. It is inevitable that an asteroid eventually slams into Earth and we are simply not prepared for it. It is inevitable that another pandemic sweeps the globe and we are simply not prepared for it.

So for those with eyes to see and ears to hear, the ancient stories have a wealth of information to share. It is up to each of us to make the necessary decisions that will decide whether the genetic heritage we inherited from our courageous ancestors will continue into the future or get snuffed out at the next catastrophe. The only guarantee is that the next catastrophe will certainly come and will, like a thief in the night, likely come unexpectedly. What one does with this awareness will, of course, determine much.

Afterword

This book started out as a series of articles on my website 2012Quest.com. It then evolved into a four part e-book series published on the Kindle platform entitled *Mayan Calendar Prophecies*. The e-books in this series were:

- Part 1: Predictions for 2012 and Beyond
- Part 2: 2012 New Age of Disasters
- Part 3: Cycle of Cosmic Catastrophes
- Part 4: The 2012 Prophecy

The e-books were then bundled into one e-book entitled *Mayan Calendar Prophecies: The Complete Collection of 2012 Prophecies and Predictions*.

After many requests for a print edition along with the fact that I had made many new discoveries after the initial publishing of the e-book series I decided to publish this volume, *Mayan Calendar Prophecies: Predictions for 2012-2052*.

My research on this topic continues. If you are interested in reading more of my research on the Mayan prophecies visit my website TheRealMayanProphecies.com or if you are interested in learning more about the ancient civilizations of the Americas visit my website, LostWorlds.org or purchase/download/rent my DVD *Lost Worlds: Georgia*.

To stay on top of the latest archaeological news and find out about my latest research, sign up for my free newsletters at http://therealmayanprophecies.com/subscribe and/or http://lostworlds.org/subscribe.

You can also "like" my TheRealMayanProphecies Facebook page at https://www.facebook.com/pages/The-

Real-Mayan-Prophecies/236972859695421 or my LostWorlds Facebook page at https://www.facebook.com/lostworlds

Author's Note

There is an ongoing debate among Mayan scholars as to the correct usage of Maya versus Mayan. The overly simplified version is that Maya is reserved for the people and Mayan for the language. In this version, Maya is both a singular and plural noun as well as an adjective. Thus one would say, "Three Maya went to the store. Maya art is exquisite." Besides sounding "wrong" to the ears of the average reader this arbitrary rule presents a problem. Is a "Maya scholar" someone who studies the Maya or is he a scholar of Mayan descent? Furthermore, Mayan scholars call themselves "Mayanists." If "Mayan" refers only to the language then are "Mayanists" people who study the Mayan language? Actually, "Mayanist" refers to scholars who study any aspect of Mayan civilization thus these Mayanists do not even follow their own rule when referring to themselves.

Another group of scholars allows the use of Mayan as an adjective such as "Mayan textiles," "Mayan culture," and "Mayan scholar." This group also allows "Mayas" as a plural form of Maya, i.e. "Three Mayas went to the store." While yet another group of scholars believes that "Mayans" is the more appropriate plural form. Thus there is no real consensus even among academics as to the "proper and right" way of doing things. The reality is no scholar has been perfectly consistent in following any of these rules sometimes breaking them within a single journal article or book.

I think the overly simplified "Maya for people, Mayan for the language" is rather clunky and ignores basic rules of English grammar. For instance, we don't say "America art" in English. We say "American art." Likewise, the average person does not search for "Maya calendar" on the Internet. They search for "Mayan calendar." To the average person "Mayan Calendar" sounds "right" as opposed to "Maya calendar." More importantly, using "Mayan" as an adjective allows for a distinction between someone who simply studies the Maya (a Mayan scholar) and someone who is a Maya with an advanced degree (a Maya scholar.) It also makes it clear that a "Mayanist" is a person who studies the ancient Maya as opposed to someone who simply studies the language only.

For all of these reasons I will use "Mayan" in reference to the language as well as an adjective throughout this text. It should be abundantly clear from the context when I'm referring to the language and when I'm using it as an adjective. But I will use "Maya" as both a singular noun and plural. It just sounds better to my ears to say "The Maya" rather than "Mayas" or "Mayans." Others are free to use whichever method works best for them.

Appendices

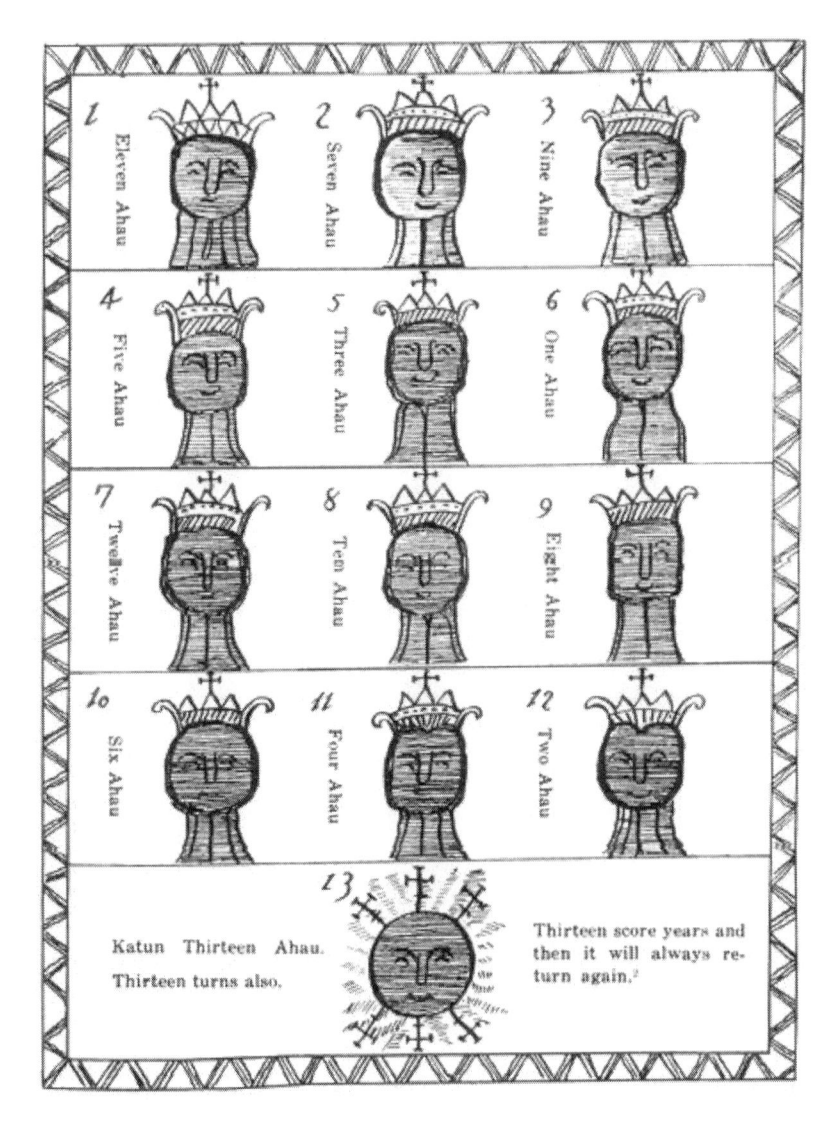

Above: The Lords of the Thirteen Katuns from the Chilam Balam of Chumayel

A. Witches, Dragons, Halloween & Christmas

The Taurid meteor shower occurs every fall in October and November. Its name originates from the fact that the meteors appear to emanate from the Pleiades star group within the constellation Tauris, thus Taurids. It is caused by the Earth traveling through a section of space previously traversed by comet Encke. As the debris from this comet in the form of dust and pebble-sized fragments burn up in the atmosphere they create what we call shooting or falling stars. Sometimes meteors can give off a green glow due to the presence of magnesium or nickel in their composition.

The height or most active period of this shower is around Halloween. Halloween fireballs or bolides are not uncommon. These are larger baseball and basketball-sized meteors that take longer to burn up in the atmosphere. These appear as balls of fire streaking through the sky with long trails of smoke following behind them.

Halloween or "All Hallowed Evening" was the evening before All Saints Day, a holiday originally associated with the returning souls of the previously departed. Since many cultures saw stars as the resting place of souls after death it was only logical that falling stars were viewed as the souls of the dead returning to Earth. This explains why Halloween and All Saints Day/All Souls Day were celebrated at the end of October, beginning of November during the height of the Taurid meteor shower.

The fact that some of these comet fragments burn green as they fly across the sky is likely the origin behind the belief in green witches flying through the sky on broomsticks on Halloween. Comets were referred to as "broom stars" in some cultures because of their broom-like appearance. Thus comet fragments burning green in the atmosphere became symbolized as green witches riding broomsticks across the sky. Curiously, witches are usually depicted wearing a pointed hat. Just such a hat was unearthed in one of the Tocharian graves discussed in chapter 20. Could the appearance of such a hat on modern witches be a faded memory of the Tocharians who likely spread these myths around the world?

Fireballs or bolides are also the likely origin behind the myth of fire-breathing dragons. Dragons were seen as serpents that flew across the sky thus the earliest depictions of dragons were as a snake with wings. Later this evolved into a creature with legs as well. The fact that these dragons "breathed fire" likely originated from the flames at the front of the meteor as it burned in the atmosphere. Thus this flaming meteor with a long smoky tail became symbolized as a fire-breathing dragon.

As noted in chapter 20, the Chinese and other cultures referred to constellations as "mansions" or "houses," i.e., the house of Scorpio, the house of Leo, etc. Since these "mansions" are composed of stars and stars were seen as the place souls go after death it then followed logically that the souls of the dead lived in mansions in the sky. This is likely the origin of the Christian belief in heavenly mansions awaiting the souls of the faithful after death.

As mentioned in chapter 8, comets were often represented as an old man with a long beard wearing a long robe. Curiously, Father Christmas was also represented as an old man with a long beard wearing a robe. In the earliest depictions of Father Christmas he is wearing a green robe not a red one. Could Father Christmas represent the same green comet, Comet Machholz, as does the Kukulkan-Quetzalcoatl myth?

Father Christmas wearing a long green robe.

The myths surrounding Father Christmas are quite interesting. Father Christmas was said to live at the North Pole. He was said to always be watching and recording the good and bad deeds of children. It was said he would deliver his judgment to these children on Christmas, December 25th. He would deliver this judgment on a sleigh pulled by reindeer. Sometimes this was a magical sleigh that flew through the sky. Other times he was said to ride a Yule goat which was itself a reference to the goats that pulled Thor's chariot through the sky.[191]

The fact that Father Christmas resided at the North Pole immediately associates him with the North Star and thus with astronomy. The North Star being the only star that never sets makes it the perfect all-seeing, all knowing "eye-in-the-sky." Again, the myths appear to encode astronomical information. This is similar to the Mayan Flood Myth discussed in chapter 15 where the constellation Draco, home to the North Star Thuban in 3300 BC, oversaw all the events recorded in that particular myth.

The fact that Father Christmas rode a sleigh pulled by reindeer or rode a goat associates him with the constellation Taurus, the only constellation that visibly looks like a horned animal. The long green robe and long beard of Father Christmas further associates him with a comet particularly a green comet.

Thus the symbolism of the Father Christmas myth suggests he is a green comet associated with the constellation Taurus who will deliver judgment to the Earth's children on December 25th.

As discussed in chapter 8, on December 7, 2004 the green comet Machholz first became naked eye visible. Its tail entered the Pleiades asterism in the constellation Taurus a month later on January 7, 2005.

While comet Machholz was passing near the Pleiades, on December 27, 2004 one of the most powerful gamma ray bursts ever recorded was measured on Earth. It originated from the magnetar SGR-1806 in the constellation Sagittarius near the Galactic Center.[192]

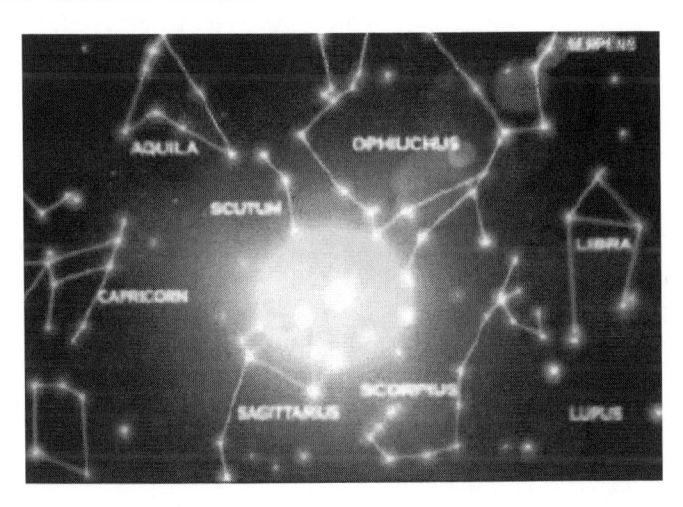

SGR-1806 is an ultra-magnetic neutron star, called a magnetar, located about 50,000 light years away from Earth in the constellation Sagittarius. (Courtesy NASA)

Physicist Dr. Paul LaViolette theorized that the energy from the gamma ray burst would have been preceded by a gravity wave 24 hours earlier on December 26th. The arrival time of this gravity wave coincided with one of the largest earthquakes ever recorded: the Indonesian megaquake. This earthquake created an enormous tsunami that killed over 240,000 people worldwide on December 26, 2004. (Most of the world received this news on December

25th since the event happened at 00 hours 58 minutes Universal Time which made it still December 25th in much of the world. For instance, in Hawaii it was 3:00 PM on December 25, 2004 when the news of the earthquake was first reported.[193])

Thus judgment was delivered to the world's children on December 25th as a green comet passed near the constellation Taurus just as the Father Christmas mythology suggested.

Is this coincidence or did someone design the myth of Father Christmas to warn future generations of a catastrophe on December 25th when a green comet was in the constellation of Taurus? If the legend of Father Christmas was truly created to warn of this disaster it suggests an astronomically sophisticated civilization existed in the past and our modern myths and legends preserve their knowledge.

As noted in chapter 21, the Aztec Calendar Stone featured star patterns carved into the left flange of the sculpture which one astronomer interpreted as a representation of the Milk Ladle asterism within the constellation Sagittarius. Strangely, the Aztec Calendar Stone states that the Fifth World would end due to earthquakes. Did they somehow know that a star in the constellation Sagittarius was capable of creating devastating earthquakes on Earth? Is this also why the English word 'disaster' literally means "bad star?" Would the Aztecs have interpreted this event as the end of the Fifth Sun and beginning of a new age just as they believed the Fourth Sun ended in 1011 AD after the appearance of a supernova in Sagittarius followed by an impact event?

Whether Father Christmas was really meant to relay a message to the future about a disaster on December 25th or not, one thing that is common in all these ancient myths is that disasters were seen as the judgment of God. The survivors saw themselves as somehow chosen and saw the victims as somehow sinners who deserved their fate. The Biblical character of Samson discussed in chapter 18 was the final "judge" recorded in the Book of Judges. Thus the ancient concept of "judgment day" was equivalent to "mega-disaster."

As the examples above reveal, much of mythology and even modern religion has an astronomical origin. Unfortunately many Mayanists insist on a literal interpretation of Mayan myths just as their counterparts in conservative religious sects insist on literal interpretations of the Bible. Ignoring the astronomical underpinnings of these myths results in interpretations that are nonsensical and makes the Maya seem superstitious and backwards depriving them of their true scientific accomplishments.

B. Creation Story from the Chilam Balam of Chumayel

Chapter X. The Creation of the World

It is most necessary to believe this. These are the precious stones which our Lord, the Father, has abandoned. This was his first repast, this balché, with which we, the ruling men revere him here. Very rightly they worshipped as true gods these precious stones, when the true God was established, our Lord God, the Lord of heaven and earth, the true God. Nevertheless, the first gods were perishable gods. Their worship came to its inevitable end. They lost their efficacy by the benediction of the Lord of Heaven, after the redemption of the world was accomplished, after the resurrection of the true God, the true Dios, when he blessed heaven and earth. Then was your worship abolished, Maya men. Turn away your hearts from your <old> religion.

<This is> the history of the world in those times, because it has been written down, because the time has not yet ended for making these books, these many explanations, so that Maya men may be asked if they know how they were born here in this country, when the land was founded.

It was <Katun> 11 Ahau when the Ah Mucenca came forth to blindfold the faces of the Oxlahun-ti-ku; but they did not know his name, except for his older sister and his sons. They said his face had not yet been shown to them also. This was after the creation of the world had been completed, but they did not know it was about to occur. Then Oxlahun-ti-ku was seized by Bolon-ti-ku. Then it was that fire descended, then the rope descended, then rocks and trees descended. Then came the beating of <things> with wood and stone.

Then Oxlahun-ti-ku / was seized, his head was wounded, his face was buffeted, he was spit upon, and he was <thrown> on his back as well. After that he was despoiled of his insignia and his smut. Then shoots of the yaxum tree were taken. Also Lima beans were taken with crumbled tubercles, hearts of small squash-seeds, large squash-seeds and beans, all crushed. He wrapped up the seeds <composing> this first Bolon ¢acab, and went to the thirteenth heaven. Then a mass of maize-dough with the tips of corn-cobs remained here on earth. Then its heart departed because of Oxlahun-ti-ku, but they did not know the heart of the tubercle was gone. After that the fatherless ones, the miserable ones, and those without husbands were all pierced through; they were alive though they had no hearts. Then they were buried in the sands, in the sea.

There would be a sudden rush of water when the theft of the insignia <of Oxlahun-ti-ku> occurred. Then the sky would fall, it would fall down upon the earth, when the four gods, the four Bacabs, were set up, who brought about the destruction of the world. Then, after the destruction of the world was completed, they placed <a tree > to set up in its order the yellow cock oriole. Then the white tree of abundance was set up. A pillar of the sky was set up, a sign of the destruction of the world; that was the white tree of abundance in the north. Then the black tree of abundance was set up <the west> for the black-breasted pi¢oy to sit upon. Then the yellow tree of abundance was set up <in the south>, as a symbol of the destruction of the world, for the yellow-breasted pi¢oy to sit upon, for the yellow cock oriole to sit upon, the yellow timid mut. Then the green tree of abundance was set up in the center <of the world> as a record of the destruction of the world.

The plate of another katun was set up and fixed in its place by the messengers of their lord. The red Piltec was set at the east of the world to conduct people to his lord. The white Piltec was set at the north of the world to conduct people / to his lord. Lahun Chaan was set <at the west> to bring things to his lord. The yellow Piltec was set <at the south> to bring things to his lord. But it was <over> the whole world that Ah Uuc Cheknal was set up. He came from the seventh stratum of the earth, when he came to fecundate Itzam-kab-ain, when he came with the vitality of the angle between earth <and> heaven. They moved among the four lights, among the four layers of the stars. The world was not lighted; there was neither day nor night nor moon. Then they perceived that the world was being created. Then creation dawned upon the world. ✠ During the creation thirteen infinite series <added> to seven was the count of the creation of the world. Then a new world dawned for them.

The two-day throne was declared, the three-day throne. Then began the weeping of Oxlahun-ti-ku. They wept in this reign. The reign became red; the mat became red; the first tree of the world was rooted fast. The entire world was proclaimed by Uuc-yol-zip; but it was not at the time of this reign that Bolon-ti-ku-wept. Then came the counting of the mat in its order. Red was the mat on which Bolon-ti-ku sat. His buttock is sharply rounded, as he sits on his mat. Then descended greed from the heart of the sky, greed for power, greed for rule.

Then the red foundation was established; the white foundation of the ruler was established; the black foundation was established; the yellow foundation was established. Then the Red Ruler was set up, he who was raised upon the mat, raised upon the throne. The White Ruler was set up, he who was raised upon the mat, raised upon the throne. The Black Ruler was set up, he who was raised upon the mat, raised upon the throne. The Yellow Ruler was set up, he who was raised upon the mat, raised upon the throne. As a god, it is said; whether or not gods, their bread is lacking, their water is lacking. /

There was only a portion <of what was needed> for them to eat together...but there was nowhere from which the quantity needed for existence could come. Compulsion and force were the tidings, when he was seated <in authority>; compulsion was the tidings, compulsion by misery; it came during his reign, when he arrived to sit upon the mat ... Suddenly on high fire flamed up. The face of the sun was snatched away, taken from earth. This was his garment in his reign. This was the reason for mourning his power, at that time there was too much vigor. At that time there was the riddle for the rulers. The planted timber was set up. Perishable things are assembled at that time. The timber of the grave-digger is set up at the crossroads, at the four resting places. Sad is the general havoc, at that time the butterflies swarmed. Then there came great misery, when it came about that the sun in Katun 3 Ahau was moved from its place for three months. After three years it will come back into place in Katun 3 Ahau. Then another katun will beset <in its place>. The ramon fruit is their bread, the ramon fruit is their drink; the jícama cimarrona is their bread, the jícama cimarrona is their drink; what they eat and what they drink. The ix-batun, the chimchim-chay, are what they eat. These things were present here when misery settled, father, in Tun. At that time there were the foreigners. The charge <of misery> was sought for all the years of <Katun> 13 Ahau.

Then it was that the lord of <Katun> 11 Ahau spread his feet apart. Then it was that the word of Bolon ¢acab descended to the tip of his tongue. Then the charge of the katun was sought; nine was its charge when it descended from heaven. Kan was the day when its burden was bound to it. Then the water descended, it came from the heart of the sky for the baptism of the House of Nine Bushes. With it descended Bolon Mayel; sweet was his mouth and the tip of his tongue. Sweet were his brains. Then descended the four mighty supernatural jars, this was the honey of the flowers. / Then there grew up for it the red unfolded calyx, the white unfolded calyx, the black unfolded calyx and the yellow unfolded calyx, those which were half a palm <broad> and those which were a whole palm <in breadth>. Then there sprang up the five-leafed 10 flower, the five drooping <petals>, the cacao <with grains like> a row of teeth, the ix-chabil-tok, the little flower, Ix Macuil Xuchit, the flower with the brightly colored tip, the laurel flower, and the limping flower. After these flowers sprang up, there were the vendors of fragrant odors, there was the mother of the flowers. Then there sprang up the bouquet of the priest, the bouquet of the ruler, the bouquet of the captain; this was what the flower-king bore when he descended and nothing else, so they say. It was not bread that he bore. Then it was that the flower sprang up, wide open, to introduce the sin of Bolon-ti-ku. <After> three years was the time when he said he did not come to create Bolon ¢acab as the god in hell. Then descended Ppizlimtec to take the flower; he took the figure of a humming-bird with green plumage on its breast, when he descended. Then he sucked the honey from the flower with nine petals. Then the five-petaled flower took him for her husband, Thereupon the heart of the flower came forth to set itself in motion. Four-fold was the plate of the flower, and Ah Kin Xocbiltun was set in the center. At this time Oxlahun-ti-ku came forth, but he did not know of the descent of the sin of the mat, when he came into his power. The flower was his mat, the flower was his chair. He sat in envy, he walked in envy. Envy was his plate, envy was his cup. There was envy in his heart, in his understanding, in his thought and in his speech. Ribald and insolent was his speech during his reign. At that time his food cries out, his drink cries out, from the corner of his mouth when he eats, from the back of his claw when he bites his food. He holds in his hand a piece of wood, he holds in his hand a stone. Mighty are his teeth; his face is that of Lahun Chan, as he sits. Sin is <in> his face, in his speech, in his talk, in his understanding <and in> his walk. His eyes are blindfolded. He seizes, he demands as his right, the mat on which he sits

/ during his reign. Forgotten is his father, forgotten is his mother, nor does his mother know her offspring. The heart is on fire alone in the fatherless one who despises his father, in the motherless one. He shall walk abroad giving the appearance of one drunk, without understanding, in company with his father, in company with his mother. There is no virtue in him, there is no goodness in his heart, only a little on the tip of his tongue. He does not know in what manner his end is to come; nor does he know what will be the end of his reign, when the period of his power shall terminate.

This is Bolon-ti-ku. <Like that of> Bolon Chan is the face of the ruler of men, the two day occupant of the mat and throne. He came in Katun 3 Ahau. After that there will be another lord of the land who will establish the law of another katun, after the law of the lord of Katun 3 Ahau shall have run its course. At that time there shall be few children; then there shall be mourning among the Itza who speak our language brokenly. Industry <and> vigor finally take the place, in the first tun <of the new katun>, of the sin of the Itzá who speak our language brokenly. It is Bolon-ti-ku who shall come to his end <with> the law of the lord of Katun 3 Ahau. Then the riddle of the rulers of the land shall end the law of the katun. Then those of the lineage of the noble chiefs shall come into their own, with the other men of discretion and with those of the lineage of the chiefs. Their faces had been trampled on the ground, and they had been overthrown by the unrestrained upstarts of the day and of the katun, the son of evil and the offspring of the harlot, who were born when their day dawned in Katun 3 Ahau. Thus shall end the power of those who are two-faced toward our Lord God.

But when the law of the katun shall have run its course, then God will bring about a great deluge again which will be the end of the world. When this is over, then our Lord Jesus Christ shall descend over the valley of Jehoshaphat beside the town of Jerusalem / where he redeemed us with his holy blood. He shall descend on a great cloud to bear true testimony that he was once obliged to suffer, stretched out on a cross of wood. Then shall descend in his great power and glory the true God who created heaven and earth and everything on earth. He shall descend to level off the world for the good and the bad, the conquerors <and> the captives.

C. The Katun Prophecies from the Chilam Balam of Chumayel

There are multiple versions of the katun prophecies in the *Chilam Balam of Chumayel* as translated by Ralph Roys. These prophecies are recorded in chapters 18, 22, & 24 of his translation. Below you will find all of these versions for the three *katun* periods covered in this book, *katuns* 4, 2 and 13. Use them to understand what type of events the Maya believed were cyclical and thus predictable.

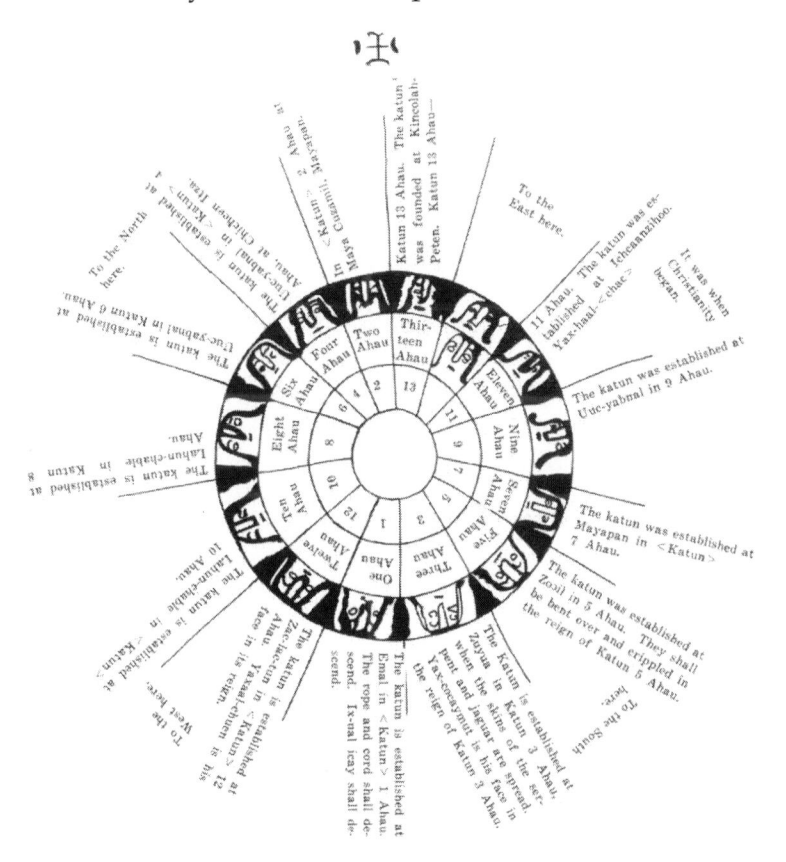

Image: The Katun Wheel from the *Chilam Balam of Chumayel*

Chapter XVIII A Series of Katun Prophecies

Katun 4 Ahau

The katun is established at Uuc-yab-nal in Katun 4 Ahau. At the mouth of the well, Uuc-yab-nal, it is established ... It shall dawn in the south. The face of <the lord of the katun> is covered; his face is dead. There is mourning for water; there is mourning for bread. His mat and his throne shall face the west. Blood-vomit is the charge <of the katun>. At that time his loin-cloth and his mantle shall be white. Unattainable shall be the bread of the katun. The quetzal shall come; the green bird shall come. The kax tree shall come; the bird shall come. The tapir shall come. The tribute shall be hidden at the mouth of the well.

Katun 2 Ahau

The katun is established at Maylu, Zaci, Mayapan in Katun 2 Ahau. The katun <stone> is on its own base. The rope shall descend; the poison of the serpent shall descend, pestilence <and> three piles of skulls. The men are of little use. Then the burden was bound on Buluc-chabtan. <Then there came up> a dry wind. The ramon is the bread of <Katun> 2 Ahau. It shall be half famine and half abundance. This is the charge of Katun 2 Ahau.

Katun 13 Ahau

The Katun is established at Kinchil Coba, Maya Cuzamil, in Katun 13 Ahau. Itzamna, Itzam-tzab, is his face during its reign. The ramon shall be eaten. Three years shall be locust years, ten generations <of locusts>. The fan shall be displayed; the bouquet shall be displayed, borne by Yaxaal Chac in the heavens. Unattainable is the bread of the katun in 13 Ahau. The sun shall be eclipsed. Double is the charge of the katun: men without offspring, chiefs without successors. For five days the sun shall be eclipsed, then it shall be seen <again>. This is the charge of Katun 13 Ahau.

Chapter XXII A Book of Katun Prophecies

Katun 4 Ahau

Katun 4 Ahau is the eleventh katun according to the count. The katun is established at Chichen Itzá. The settlement of the Itzá shall take place <there>. The quetzal shall come, the green bird shall come. Ah Kantenal shall come. Blood-vomit shall come. Kukulcan shall come with them for the second time. <It is> the word of God. The Itzá shall come.

Katun 2 Ahau

Katun 2 Ahau is the twelfth katun. At Maya [uaz] Cuzamil the katun is established. For half <the katun> there will be bread; for half <the katun> there will be water. <It is> the word of God. For half of it there will be a temple for the rulers. <It is> the end of the word of God.

Katun 13 Ahau

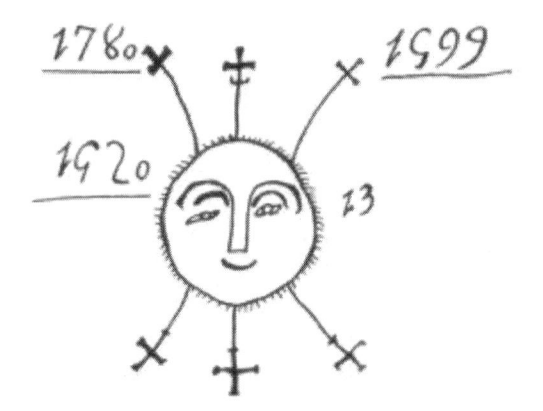

The judgment.

It is Katun 13 Ahau according to the count. The katun is established at Kinchil Coba, the thirteenth katun. The bouquet of the rulers of the world shall be displayed. There is the universal judgment of our Lord God. Blood shall descend from the tree and stone. Heaven and earth shall burn. It is the word of God the Father, God the Son and God the Holy Spirit. It is the holy judgment, the holy judgment of our Lord God. There shall be no strength in heaven and earth. Great cities shall enter into Christianity, any settlements of people whatever, the great towns, whatever their names are as well as the little towns, all over our land of Maya Cuzamil Mayapan. <It shall be> for our two-day men, because of lewdness . . . the sons of malevolence. At the end of our blindness and shame our sons shall be regenerated from carnal sin. There is no lucky day for us. It is the cause of death from bad blood, when the moon rises, when the moon sets, the entire moon, <this was> its power; <it was> all blood. So it was with the good planets <which were> looked upon as good. It is the end of the word of God. The waters of baptism shall come over them, the Holy Spirit. They receive the holy oil without compulsion; it comes from God. There are too many Christians who go to those who deny the holy faith, . . . <to> the Itzá and the balams. There is then an end to our losing...

Chapter XXIV Prophecies of a New Religion

Katun 4 Ahau

The prophecy of Nahau Pech the great priest. At that time when the sun shall stand high <in the heavens>, lord, when the ruler has had compassion, in the fourth katun it shall come to pass, the tidings of God are truly brought. They ask perchance what I recommend, lord. You see your guests upon the road, oh Itzá! It is the fathers of the land who will arrive. <This prophecy> comes from the mouth of Nahau Pech, the priest in the time of Katun 4 Ahau at the end of the

katun, lord. The food of the ant<-like> men shall be destroyed. They shall be at the end of their food <-supply> because of the boboch <which takes their> food, the great hawk <which takes their> food, the ant, the cowbird, the grackle, the blackbird, the mouse.

Katun 13 Ahau

The prophecy of Chilam Balam, the singer, of Cabal-chen, Mani. On <the day> 13 Ahau the katun will end in the time of the Itzá, in the time of Tancah <Mayapan>, lord. There is the sign of Hunab-ku on high. The raised wooden standard shall come. It shall be displayed to the world, that the world may be enlightened, lord.

There has been a beginning of strife, there has been a beginning of rivalry, when the priestly man shall come to bring the sign <of God> in time to come, lord. A quarter of a league, a league <away> he comes. You see the mut-bird surmounting the raised wooden standard. A new day shall dawn in the north, in the west.

Itzamná Kauil shall rise. Our lord comes, Itzá. Our elder brother comes, <oh> men of Tantun. Receive your guests, the bearded men, the men of the east, the bearers of the sign of God, lord. Good indeed is the word of God that comes to us. The day of our regeneration comes. You do not fear the world, Lord, you are the only God who created us. It is sufficient, then, that the word of God is good, lord. <He is> the guardian of our souls. He who receives him, who has truly believed, he will go to heaven with him. Nevertheless <at> the beginning were the two-day men.

Let us exalt his sign on high, let us exalt it <that we may gaze upon it today> with the raised standard. Great is the discord that arises today. The First Tree of the World is restored; it is displayed to the world. This is the sign of Hunab-ku on high. Worship it, Itzá. You shall worship today his sign on high. You shall worship it furthermore with true good will, and you shall worship the true God today, lord. You shall be converted to the word of Hunab-ku, lord; it came from heaven. Oh it is he who speaks to you! Be admonished indeed, Itzá. They will correct their ways who receive him in their hearts in another katun, lord.

Believe in my word itself, I am Chilam Balam, and I have interpreted the entire message of the true God <of> the world; it is heard in every part of the world, lord, the word of God, the Lord of heaven and earth. Very good indeed is his word in heaven, lord. He is ruler over us; he is the true God over our souls.

But those to whom <the word> is brought, lord: thrice weighed down is their strength, the younger brothers native to the land. Their hearts are submerged <in sin>. Their hearts are dead in their carnal sins. They are frequent backsliders, the principal ones who spread <sin>, Nacxit Xuchit in the carnal sin of his companions, the two-day rulers. <They sit> crookedly on their thrones; crookedly in carnal sin. Two-day men they call them. For two days <endure> their seats, their cups, their hats. They are the unrestrained lewd ones of the day, the unrestrained lewd ones of the night, the rogues of the world. They twist their necks, they wink their eyes, they slaver at the mouth, at the rulers of the land, lord. Behold, when they come, there is no truth in the words of the foreigners to the land. They tell very solemn and mysterious things, the sons of the men of Seven-deserted-buildings, the offspring of the women of Seven-deserted-buildings, lord.

Who will be the prophet, who will be the priest who shall interpret truly the word of the book?

D. The Mayan Chronicles from the Chilam Balam of Chumayel

Within the *Chilam Balam of Chumayel* translated by Ralph Roys were a series of chronicles or histories recorded for each *katun*. The Maya believed that what happened in one *katun* could happen again when the *katun* returned in the future. Since each named *katun* reoccurred every 256 years, the Maya priests wanted to keep track of events in each *katun* in order to detect patterns in each *katun* from which they could make more accurate predictions about the future. This is little different than modern forecasting.

Below you will find the events which the Maya recorded as happening in previous *katuns*. I've only included events for the three *katun* periods covered by this book: *katuns* 4, 2 and 13. If the *katun* is blank then that means nothing was recorded for this *katun*. Since each *katun* cycle consisted of 256 years and there are five *katun* cycles for which events were recorded, these chronicles cover around 1200 years of Maya history.

Chapter XIX The First Chronicle

4 Ahau.

2 Ahau.

13 Ahau was when the mat <of the katun> was counted in order.

4 Ahau was when the land was seized by them at Chakanputun.

2 Ahau.

13 Ahau.

4 Ahau.

2 Ahau.

13 Ahau.

4 Ahau was when the land of Ich-paa Mayapan was seized by the Itzá men who had been separated from their homes because of the people of Izamal and because of the treachery of Hunac Ceel.

2 Ahau.

13 Ahau.

4 Ahau was when the pestilence occurred; it was when the vultures entered the houses within the fortress.

2 Ahau was when the eruption of pustules occurred. It was smallpox.

13 Ahau was when the rain-bringer died. It was the sixth year. The year-count was to the east. It was <the year> 4 Kan. Pop was set to the east. . . . It was the <fif>teenth <day of the month> Zip. 9 Imix was the day when the rain-bringer, Napot Xiu, died. It was the year of our Lord 158.

Chapter XX The Second Chronicle

4 Ahau was the name of the katun when occurred the birth of Pauahs, when the rulers descended.

Thirteen katuns they reigned; thus they were named while they ruled.

4 Ahau was the name of the katun when they descended; the great descent and the little descent they were called.

Thirteen katuns they reigned. So they were called. While they were settled, thirteen were their settlements.

4 Ahau was the katun when they sought and discovered Chichen Itzá. There it was that miraculous things were performed for them by their lords. Four divisions they were, when the four divisions of the nation, as they were called, went forth. From Kincolahpeten in the east one division went forth. From Nacocob in the north one division came forth. But one division came forth from Holtun Zuyua in the west. One division came forth from Four-peaked Mountain, Nine Mountains is the name of the land.

4 Ahau was the katun when the four divisions were called <together>. The four

divisions of the nation, they were called, when they descended. They became lords when they descended upon Chichen Itzá. The Itzá were they then called.

Thirteen katuns they ruled, and then came the treachery by Hunac Ceel. Their town was abandoned and they went into the heart of the forest to Tan-xuluc-mul, as it is called.

4 Ahau was the katun when their souls cried out!

Thirteen katuns they ruled in their misery!

13 Ahau was the katun when they founded the town of Mayapan, the Maya men, as they were called.

Chapter XXI The Third Chronicle

A record of the katuns for the Itzá, called the Maya katuns.

4 Ahau.

2 Ahau.

13 Ahau.

4 Ahau.

2 Ahau.

13 Ahau.

4 Ahau. The stone was taken at Atikuh. This was the katun when the pestilence

occurred. It was in the fifth tun of Katun 4 Ahau.

2 Ahau. The stone was taken at Chacalna.

13 Ahau. The stone was taken at Euan.

On this 18th day of August, 1766, occurred a hurricane. I have made a record of it in order that it may be seen how many years it will be before another one will occur.*

(Author's Note: 1766 occurred during a katun 4 ahau cycle, thus I've included this passage here.)

On this 20th day of January, 1782, there was an epidemic of inflammation here in the town of Chumayel. The swelling began at the neck and then descended. <It spread> from the little ones to the adults, until it swept the entire house, once it was introduced. The remedy was sour ashes and lemons or the young Siempre vive. It was the year of '81 when it began. After that there was a great drought also. There was scarcely any rain. The entire forest was burned <with the heat>, and the forest <trees> died This is the record which I have written down, I, Don Juan Josef Hoil. (Rubrica.)*

(Author's Note: 1782 occurred during a katun 13 ahau cycle, thus I've included this passage here.)

References

[1] "Foundation for the Study of Cycles." FoundationForTheStudyofCycles.org. Accessed online 18 August 2012 at <http://www.foundationforthestudyofcycles.org/>.
[2] "Foundation for the Study of Cycles." FoundationForTheStudyofCycles.org. Accessed online 18 August 2012 at <http://www.foundationforthestudyofcycles.org/>.
[3] "Earthquakes, Tsunami's, and the Seismic Cycle." Tectonics.CalTech.edu. Accessed online 12 September 2012 at <http://www.tectonics.caltech.edu/outreach/animations/subduction_youtube.html>.
[4] Vaquero, J.M. "A 250-year cycle in naked-eye observations of sunspots." *GEOPHYSICAL RESEARCH LETTERS*, VOL. 29, 1997, 4 PP., 2002. Accessed online 4 September 2012 at <http://www.agu.org/pubs/crossref/2002/2002GL014782.shtml>.
[5] Asher, D. J., et al. "Earth in the Cosmic Shooting Gallery." *Observatory*. Accessed online 21 October 2012 at <http://articles.adsabs.harvard.edu/cgi-bin/nph-iarticle_query?2005Obs...125..319A&data_type=PDF_HIGH&whole_paper=YES&type=PRINTER&filetype=.pdf>.
[6] Baille, Mike. *New Light on the Black Death: The Cosmic Connection*. Tempus, 2006, p.199.
[7] "Tunguska event." Wikpedia.org. <http://en.wikipedia.org/wiki/Tunguska_event>.
[8] Finsinger, Walter and Willy Tinner. "Holocene vegetation and land use changes in response to climatic changes in the forelands of the southwestern Alps, Italy." *Journal of Quaternary Science*. Wiley InterScience. 2006: Vol. 1, pp. 243-258. Accessed online 16 August 2012 at <http://igitur-archive.library.uu.nl/bio/2008-0930-200335/Finsinger_06_Holocene vegetation.pdf>.
[9] Vaquero, J.M. "Sunspot numbers can detect pandemic influenza A: The use of different sunspot numbers."
[10] Hayes, Daniel P. "Influenza pandemics, solar activity cycles, and vitamin D." *Medical Hypotheses*. 2010 May;74(5):831-4. Accessed online 4 September 2012 at <http://www.vitamindwiki.com/tiki-download_file.php?fileId=201>.

[11] Hayes, Daniel P. "Influenza pandemics, solar activity cycles, and vitamin D." *Medical Hypotheses*. 2010 May;74(5):831-4. Accessed online 4 September 2012 at <http://www.vitamindwiki.com/tiki-download_file.php?fileId=201>.

[12] Hayes, Daniel P. "Influenza pandemics, solar activity cycles, and vitamin D." *Medical Hypotheses*. 2010 May;74(5):831-4. Accessed online 4 September 2012 at <http://www.vitamindwiki.com/tiki-download_file.php?fileId=201>.

[13] Davis, G. E., Jr. "Solar cycles and their relationship to human disease and adaptability." *Medical Hypotheses*. 2006;67(3):447-61. Accessed online 5 September 2012 at <http://www.ncbi.nlm.nih.gov/pubmed/16701959>.

[14] Raps, Avi, et al; "Geophysical Variables and Behavior: LXIX. Solar Activity and Admission of Psychiatric Inpatients," *Perceptual and Motor Skills*, 74:449, 1992.

[15] Randall, Walter, and Randall, Steffani; "The Solar Wind and Hallucinations--- A Possible Relation Due to Magnetic Disturbances," *Bioelectromagnetics*, 12: 67, 1991.

[16] Ertel, Suitbert; "Synchronous Bursts of Creativity in Independent Cultures; Evidence for an Extraterrestrial Connection," *The Explorer*, 5:12, Fall 1989.

[17] "Alexander_Chizhevsky." Wikipedia.org. Accessed online 5 September 2012 at <http://en.wikipedia.org/wiki/Alexander_Chizhevsky>.

[18] Dewey, Edward R. "Stocks and space." *Cycles*. Foundation for the Study of Cycles. October 1969. Accessed online 5 September 2012 at <http://cycles.cc/24K-7.htm>.

[19] Abazajian, Kevork. "Gamma rays from galactic center could be evidence of dark matter." *Physical Review D*. American Physical Society. Accessed online 8 September 2012 at <http://today.uci.edu/news/2012/08/nr_darkmatter_120813.php>.

[20] Makemson, Maud Worcester. *The Book of the Jaguar Priest*. New York: 1951, p. 217.

[21] Roys, Ralph. *The Chilam Balam of Chumayel*.

[22] Reindorp, Reginald & Eugene R. Craine, translators. *The Codex Perez and the Book of Chilam Balam of Mani*. University of Oklahoma Press: p.85.
[23] Kirkpatrick, Marshal. "Google CEO Schmidt: "People Aren't Ready for the Technology Revolution." ReadWriteWeb.com. Accessed online 22 September 2012 at <http://www.readwriteweb.com/archives/google_ceo_schmidt_people_arent_ready_for_the_tech.php>.
[24] Restall, Matthew. *Maya Conquistador*. Beacon Press: 1998, p.135. Accessed online 11 May 2011 at <http://books.google.com/books?id=vBWo5cdpnhkC&lpg=PA135&ots=fxML6wEU9D&dq=Ah Kantenal he who adulterates maize&pg=PA135 - v=onepage&q="Ah Kantenal %5Bhe who adulterates maize%5D"&f=false>.
[25] "Monoculture." Wikipedia.org. Accessed online 1 November 2012 at <http://en.wikipedia.org/wiki/Monoculture>.
[26] "Colony collapse disorder." Wikipedia.org. Accessed online 22 October 2012 at <http://en.wikipedia.org/wiki/Colony_collapse_disorder>.
[27] "Orion correlation theory." Wikipedia.org. Accessed online 22 October 2012 at <http://en.wikipedia.org/wiki/Orion_correlation_theory>.
[28] "Orion correlation theory." Wikipedia.org. Accessed online 22 October 2012 at <http://en.wikipedia.org/wiki/Orion_correlation_theory>.
[29] "Fingerprints of the Gods." Wikipedia.org. Accessed online 22 October 2012 at <http://en.wikipedia.org/wiki/Fingerprints_of_the_Gods>.
[30] "Göbekli Tepe." Wikipedia.org. Accessed online 22 October 2012 at <http://en.wikipedia.org/wiki/Göbekli_Tepe>.
[31] Frum, David. "Why 2013 will be a year of crisis." CNN.com. 3 Spetember 2012. Accessed online 8 September 2012 at <http://www.cnn.com/2012/09/03/opinion/frum-food-price-crisis/index.html?hpt=hp_c2>.
[32] Crude Oil: Uncertainty About Future Oil Supply. GAO.gov. Accessed online 15 September 2012 at <http://www.gao.gov/new.items/d07283.pdf>.

[33] "Peak oil." Wikipedia.org. Accessed online 15 September 2012 at <http://en.wikipedia.org/wiki/Peak_oil>.
[34] Tyson, Neil deGrasse. "Blowing up asteroids with NASA and Neil deGrasse Tyson." Vice.com. Accessed online 12 September 2012 at <http://motherboard.vice.com/2012/8/20/motherboard-tv-inside-nasa-s-spectacular-undersea-mission-to-save-earth-from-an-asteroid>.
[35] Baillie, Mike. *New Light on the Black Death: The Cosmic Connection.* Tempus, 2006. pp. 133-134.
[36] "Comet Machholz." Wikipedia.org. Accessed online at <http://en.wikipedia.org/wiki/Comet_Machholz>.
[37] Rao, Joe. "Doorstep Astronomy: New Comet Looking Bright." Space.com. Accessed online 10 May 2011 at < http://www.space.com/626-doorstep-astronomy-comet-bright.html>.
[38] "99942 Apophis." Wikipedia.org. Accessed online 10 May 2011 at <http://en.wikipedia.org/wiki/99942_Apophis>.
[39] Campbell, Matthew. "UMass Geologist Explains Science Behind Frequent Earthquakes." CBS3Springfield.com. Accessed online 10 May 2011 at <http://www.cbs3springfield.com/news/local/UMass--117840787.html>
[40] "Mount Yamantau." Wikipedia.org. Accessed online 10 May 2011 at <http://en.wikipedia.org/wiki/Mount_Yamantau>.
[41] Von Humboldt, Alexander. *Researches, Vol. II.* London: 1814, p. 174. Accessed online 21 May 2011 at <http://olivercowdery.com/texts/1814Hum2.htm - pg174>.
[42] *Railway locomotives and cars, Volume 3.* Accessed online 21 May 2011 at <http://books.google.com/books?id=YOc6AAAAMAAJ&lpg=PA164&ots=YBuaKorAx7&dq=modern astronomers bearded comet&pg=PA164 - v=onepage&q=modern astronomers bearded comet&f=false>.
[43] "The Great Comet of 1680." GeorgeGlazer.com. Accessed online 21 May 2011 at

<http://www.georgeglazer.com/maps/celestial/cometcel.html>.
[44] "Comets in Ancient Culture." NASA.gov. Accessed online 21 May 2011 at <http://www.nasa.gov/mission_pages/deepimpact/media/f_ancient.html>.
[45] "Comet Donati." Wikipedia.org. Accessed online 21 May 2011 at <http://en.wikipedia.org/wiki/Comet_Donati>.
[46] "Codex Magliabechiano." Wikipedia.org. Accessed online 21 May 2011 at <http://en.wikipedia.org/wiki/Codex_Magliabechiano>.
[47] "Pleiades." Wikipedia.org. Accessed online 21 May 2011 at <http://en.wikipedia.org/wiki/Pleiades_(star_cluster)>.
[48] "Comet Encounter." Spaceweather.com. Accessed online 21 May 2011 at <http://spaceweather.com/archive.php?day=10&month=01&view=view&year=2005>.
[49] "Comet Machholz." Wikipedia.org. Accessed online 21 May 2011 at <http://en.wikipedia.org/wiki/Comet_Machholz>.
[50] Stuart, David. *The Order of Days*. p. 84.
[51] "Younger Dryas." Wikipedia.org. Accessed online 21 May 2011 at <http://en.wikipedia.org/wiki/Younger_Dryas>.
[52] Choi, Charles Q. "Big Freeze: Earth Could Plunge Into Sudden Ice Age." LiveScience.com. Accessed online 21 May 2011 at <http://www.livescience.com/7981-big-freeze-earth-plunge-sudden-ice-age.html>.
[53] Garcia, Erik Velasquez. "The Maya Flood Myth and the Decapitation of the Cosmic Caiman." Accessed online 26 May 2011 at <http://www.mesoweb.com/pari/publications/journal/701/flood_e.pdf>.
[54] "Comet Cools Clovis." *Astrobiology Magazine*. Accessed online 27 May 2011 at <http://www.astrobio.net/pressrelease/2437/comet-cools-clovis>.
[55] "Solutrean theory." Wikipedia.org. Accessed online 27 May 2011 at <http://en.wikipedia.org/wiki/Solutrean_theory>.

[56] "The Deadly Sting of a Comet's Tail." *Astrobiology Magazine.* Accessed online 27 May 2011 at <http://www.astrobio.net/pressrelease/3451/the-deadly-sting-of-a-comet-tail>.

[57] Leviton, Richard. *Encyclopedia of Earth Myths.* Accessed online 6 May 2011 at <http://weiserbooksblog.com/2011/01/11/esoteric-tuesday-for-1-1-11-the-mysteries-of-quetzalcoatl/>

[58] "Xolotl, God of Sickness, Deformity, and Misfortune." Accessed online 6 May 2011 at <http://ferrebeekeeper.wordpress.com/2010/05/28/xolotl-god-of-sickness-deformity-and-misfortune/>

[59] "Quetzalcoatl." Encyclopedia Britannica Online. Accessed online 10 May 2011 at <http://www.britannica.com/EBchecked/topic/487168/Quetzalcoatl>.

60 "Hermes." Wikipedia.org. Accessed online 6 May 2011 at <http://en.wikipedia.org/wiki/Hermes>

61 Brook, Jacqueline. *Our Rock Who Art in Heaven, Hallowed Be Thy Name.*

62 Campanella, Tommaso. *Astrologicorum libri VII.* Accessed online 5 May 2011 at <http://www.antonblog.net/astrology/mundane-astrology/comet-lulin/>

63 "2004 Atlantic Hurrican Season." Wikipedia.org. Accessed online 6 May 2011 at <http://en.wikipedia.org/wiki/2004_Atlantic_hurricane_season>

64 "2004 Atlantic Hurrican Season." Wikipedia.org. Accessed online 6 May 2011 at <http://en.wikipedia.org/wiki/2004_Atlantic_hurricane_season>

65 "2004 Indian Ocean earthquake and tsunami." Wikipedia.org. Accessed online 6 May 2011 at <http://en.wikipedia.org/wiki/2004_Indian_Ocean_earthquake_and_tsunami>

66 Britt, Robert Roy. "Brightest Galactic Flash Ever Detected Hits Earth." Space.com. Accessed online 6 May 2011 at <http://www.space.com/806-brightest-galactic-flash-detected-hits-earth.html>

67 LaViolette, Paul. "Was the December 26, 2004 Indonesian Earthquake and Tusnami Caused by a Stellar Explosion 46,000 Light Years Away?" Etheric.com. Accessed online 6 May 2011 at <http://www.etheric.com/GalacticCenter/GRB.html>
68 "Solar Flare." Wikipedia.org. Accessed online 7 May 2011 at <http://en.wikipedia.org/wiki/Solar_flare>.
69 "Sickening Solar Flares." NASA.gov. Accessed online 7 May 2011 at <http://science.nasa.gov/science-news/science-at-nasa/2005/27jan_solarflares/>.
70 Winter, Paul. "Cosmic dust effecting our weather started in 2000." Handpen.com. Accessed online 11 May 2011 at <http://www.handpen.com/Bio/sun_freaks.html>.
[71] Montgomery, John. *Dictionary of Maya Hieroglyphs*. FAMSI. Accessed online 11 May 2011 at <http://research.famsi.org/montgomery_dictionary/mt_entry.php?id=1276&lsearch=a&search=>.
72 "Giant breach in Earth's magnetic field discovered." NASA.gov. Accessed online 13 May 2011 at <http://science.nasa.gov/science-news/science-at-nasa/2008/16dec_giantbreach/>.
73 Cromie, William J. "Brightening sun is warming Earth." *The Harvard Gazette*. Accessed online 8 May 2011 at <http://news.harvard.edu/gazette/1997/11.06/BrighteningSuni.html>.
74 "2005 Atlantic hurricane season." Wikipedia.org. Accessed online 7 May 2011 at <http://en.wikipedia.org/wiki/2005_Atlantic_hurricane_season>.
75 "List of natural disasters." Wikipedia.org. Accessed online 7 May 2011 at <http://en.wikipedia.org/wiki/Natural_disasters_by_death_toll>.
76 "List of natural disasters." Wikipedia.org. Accessed online 7 May 2011 at <http://en.wikipedia.org/wiki/Natural_disasters_by_death_toll>.
77 "Record 312 twisters in single day, US says." MSNBC.com. Accessed online 10 May 2011 at <http://www.msnbc.msn.com/id/42863493/ns/weather/>.

78 "Younger Dryas." Wikipedia.org. Accessed online 9 May 2011 at <http://en.wikipedia.org/wiki/Younger_Dryas>.
79 "Lake Agassiz." Wikipedia.org. Accessed online 9 May 2011 at <http://en.wikipedia.org/wiki/Lake_Agassiz>.
80 "Supernova waves rolled over mammoths." Astrobiology Magazine. Accessed online 11 May 2011 at <http://www.astrobio.net/pressrelease/1726/supernova-waves-rolled-over-mammoths>.
[81] Masse, Bruce. "Myth and Catastrophic Reality: Using Cosmogenic Mythology to Identify Cosmic Impacts and Massive Plinian Eruptions in Holocene South America." 32nd International Geological Conference. Accessed online 13 May 2011 at <http://library.lanl.gov/cgi-bin/getfile?LA-UR-04-5676sc.pdf>.
[82] Schoch, Robert. "Glass castles & fire from the sky." NewDawnMagazine.com. Accessed online 11 May 2011 at <http://www.robertschoch.com/articles/schochvitrificationnewdawnspecialissuesept2010.pdf>.
[83] "Solar storm of 1859." Wikipedia.org. Accessed online 11 May 2011 at <http://en.wikipedia.org/wiki/Solar_storm_of_1859>.
[84] "Solar storm of 1859." Wikipedia.org. Accessed online 11 May 2011 at <http://en.wikipedia.org/wiki/Solar_storm_of_1859>.
[85] Winter, Paul. "Moon craters offer evidence of 50 time greater solar flare activity in our past." Handpen.com Accesed online 11 May 2011 at <http://www.handpen.com/Bio/sun_freaks.html - 50>.
[86] Peratt, Anthony. "Characteristics for the Occurrence of a High-Current, Z-Pinch Aurora as Recorded in Antiquity." IEEE Transactions on Plasma Science. Accessed online 11 May 2011 at <http://www.scribd.com/doc/14145750/Anthony-Peratt-Characteristics-for-the-Occurrence-of-a-HighCurrent-ZPinch-Aurora-as-Recorded-in-Antiquity>.
[87] "Thoth." Wikipedia.org. Accessed online 11 May 2011 at <http://en.wikipedia.org/wiki/Thoth>.
[88] "Huracan." Wikipedia.org. Accessed online 12 May 2011 at <http://en.wikipedia.org/wiki/Huracan>.

[89] "Thoth." Wikipedia.org. Accessed online 11 May 2011 at <http://en.wikipedia.org/wiki/Thoth>.
[90] "Thoth." Greenmangatekeeper.com. Accessed online 12 May 2011 at <http://www.greenmangatekeeper.com/egthoth.htm>.
[91] "Thoth." Greenmangatekeeper.com. Accessed online 12 May 2011 at <http://www.greenmangatekeeper.com/egthoth.htm>.
[92] Smith, Frank. "The Day the World Burned." SouthernCrossReview.org. Accessed online 13 May 2011 at <http://southerncrossreview.org/6/tobadog.html>.
[93] "Thoth." Greenmangatekeeper.com. Accessed online 12 May 2011 at <http://www.greenmangatekeeper.com/egthoth.htm>.
[94] LaViolette, Paul. "The Cause of Megafaunal Extinction: Supernova or Galactic Core Outburst?" Starburstfound.org. Accessed online 12 May 2011 at <http://www.starburstfound.org/YDextinct/p1.html>.
[95] McIvor, Robert. "Star Patterns on the Aztec Calendar Stone." *Journal of the Royal Astronomical Society of Canada.* Accessed online 12 May 2011 at <http://adsabs.harvard.edu/full/2000JRASC..94...56M>.
[96] Stuart, David. *The Inscriptions from Temple XIX at Palenque.* The Pre-Columbian Art Research Institute. San Francisco: 2005, p.12.
[97] Stuart, David. *The Inscriptions from Temple XIX at Palenque.* The Pre-Columbian Art Research Institute. San Francisco: 2005, p.70.
[98] Napier, Bill & Victor Clube. *The Cosmic Serpent.* Universe Pub.
[99] Stuart, David. *The Inscriptions from Temple XIX at Palenque.* The Pre-Columbian Art Research Institute. San Francisco: 2005, p.71.
[100] Stuart, David. *The Inscriptions from Temple XIX at Palenque.* The Pre-Columbian Art Research Institute. San Francisco: 2005, p.71.
[101] Sagan, Carl and Ann Druyan. *Comet.* Ballantine Books. 1997: p.192.

[102] Phillips, Tony. "The Sun Rips Off a Comet's Tail." NASA Science News: 1 October 2007. Accessed online 14 August 2012 at <http://science.nasa.gov/science-news/science-at-nasa/2007/01oct_encke/>.
[103] Carroll, B. W.; Ostlie, D. A. *An Introduction to Modern Astrophysics*. Addison-Wesley. 1996: pp. 864–874.
[104] Stuart, David. *The Inscriptions from Temple XIX at Palenque*. The Pre-Columbian Art Research Institute. San Francisco: 2005, pp.68-69.
[105] LaViolette, Paul. "A Galactic Superwave Hazard Alert Update." Starbust Foundation. August 2009. Accessed online 3 September 2012 at <http://www.starburstfound.org/downloads/superwave/Nexus2009.pdf>.
[106] Garcia, Erik Velasquez. "The Maya Flood Myth and the Decapitation of the Cosmic Caiman." PARI Online Publications. The Pre-Columbian Art Research Institute. Accessed online 14 August 2012 at <http://www.mesoweb.com/pari/publications/journal/701/flood_e.pdf>.
[107] Garcia, Erik Velasquez. "The Maya Flood Myth and the Decapitation of the Cosmic Caiman." PARI Online Publications. The Pre-Columbian Art Research Institute. Accessed online 14 August 2012 at <http://www.mesoweb.com/pari/publications/journal/701/flood_e.pdf>.
[108] Baillie, Mike. "The case for significant numbers of extraterrestrial impacts through the late Holocene." *Journal of Quaternary Science*, Vol. 22 p. 103-104. Accessed online 18 August 2012 at <http://tsun.sscc.ru/hiwg/PABL/Baillie_2007_JQS.pdf>.
[109] Atkinson, Nancy. "Comet Elenin Could Be Disintegrating." UniverseToday.com. 29 August 2011. Accessed online at <http://www.universetoday.com/88494/comet-elenin-could-be-disintigrating/>.
[110] Lasar, Matthew. "1859's 'Great Auroral Storm'—the week the Sun touched the earth." *ArsTechnica.com*. 2 May 2012. Accessed online 16 August 2012 at

<http://arstechnica.com/science/2012/05/1859s-great-auroral-stormthe-week-the-sun-touched-the-earth/>.

[111] Green, J.; Boardsen, S.; Odenwald, S.; Humble, J.; Pazamickas, K. (2006). "Eyewitness reports of the great auroral storm of 1859". *Advances in Space Research* 38 (2): 145–154. Accessed online 16 August 2012 at <http://ntrs.nasa.gov/archive/nasa/casi.ntrs.nasa.gov/20050210157_2005210155.pdf>.

[112] Schove, D. Justin. "Sunspots, Aurorae, and Blood Rain: The Spectrum of Time." *Isis*. 1951: June, Vol. 1. Accessed online 18 August 2012 at <http://www.jstor.org/stable/226971>.

[113] Green, J.; Boardsen, S.; Odenwald, S.; Humble, J.; Pazamickas, K. (2006). "Eyewitness reports of the great auroral storm of 1859". Advances in Space Research 38 (2): 145–154. Accessed online 16 August 2012 at <http://ntrs.nasa.gov/archive/nasa/casi.ntrs.nasa.gov/20050210157_2005210155.pdf>.

[114] Wendover, Roger. *Roger of Wendover's Flowers of history, 1*. Accessed online 18 August 2012 at <http://books.google.com/books?id=k-BG_t55AHUC&ots=hMObCmbruT&dq=Roger of Wendover's Flowers of history, 1&pg=PA5 - v=onepage&q&f=false>.

[115] "Blood rain." Wikipedia.org. Accessed online 18 August 2012 at <http://en.wikipedia.org/wiki/Blood_rain>.

[116] Bryant, Edward. *Tsunami: The Underrated Hazard*. Cambridge University Press. p.259. Accessed online 18 August 2012 at <http://books.google.com/books?id=MQg4AAAAIAAJ&lpg=PA259&ots=74xdHmNVV1&dq=3300 BC tsunami&pg=PA259 - v=onepage&q=3300 BC tsunami&f=false>.

[117] Bryant, Edward. "Tsunami Chronology Supporting Late Holocene Impacts." Journal of Siberian Federal University. Accessed online 18 August 2012 at <http://elib.sfu-kras.ru/bitstream/2311/1636/1/03_.pdf>.

[118] Bryant, Edward. "Tsunami Chronology Supporting Late Holocene Impacts." *Journal of Siberian Federal University*. Accessed online 18 August 2012 at <http://elib.sfu-kras.ru/bitstream/2311/1636/1/03_.pdf>.

[119] Roys, Ralph, trans. "The Creation of the World." *Chilam Balam of Chumayel*. Accessed online 19 August 2012 at <http://www.sacred-texts.com/nam/maya/cbc/cbc15.htm>.

[120] Craine, Eugene R and Reginald C. Reindorp. *The Codex Perez and the Book of Chilam Balam of Mani*. University of Oklahoma Press, 1979: p.118.

[121] Makemson, Maud Worcester. *The Book of the Jaguar Priest*. Henry Schuman. New York: p.196.

[122] "Frequently Asked Questions About a Nuclear Blast." CDC.gov. Accessed online 1 November 2012 at <http://www.bt.cdc.gov/radiation/nuclearfaq.asp>.

[123] Vasiliev, N.V., A. F. Kovalevsky, S. A. Razin, L. E. Epiktetova (1981). *Eyewitness accounts of Tunguska (Crash).*, Section 6, Item 4. Accessed online 19 August 2012 at <http://en.wikipedia.org/wiki/Tunguska_event>.

[124] "Extreme weather events of 535-536." Wikipedia.org. Accessed online 18 August 2012 at <http://en.wikipedia.org/wiki/Extreme_weather_events_of_535%E2%80%93536>.

[125] Than, Ker. "Comet smashes triggered ancient famine." NewScientist, 07 January 2009. Accessed online 18 August 2012 at <http://www.newscientist.com/article/mg20126882.900-comet-smashes-triggered-ancient-famine.html?DCMP=OTC-rss&nsref=online-news>.

[126] Than, Ker. "Comet smashes triggered ancient famine." NewScientist, 07 January 2009. Accessed online 18 August 2012 at <http://www.newscientist.com/article/mg20126882.900-comet-smashes-triggered-ancient-famine.html?DCMP=OTC-rss&nsref=online-news>.

[127] Baillie, Mike. "The case for significant numbers of extraterrestrial impacts through the late Holocene." *Journal of Quaternary Science*, Vol. 22 p. 103-104. Accessed online 18 August 2012 at <http://tsun.sscc.ru/hiwg/PABL/Baillie_2007_JQS.pdf>.

[128] Baillie, Mike. "The case for significant numbers of extraterrestrial impacts through the late Holocene." Journal of Quaternary Science, Vol. 22 p. 103. Accessed online 17 August 2012 at <http://tsun.sscc.ru/hiwg/PABL/Baillie_2007_JQS.pdf>.

[129] Rigby, Emma; Symonds, Melissa; Ward-Thompson, Derek. "A comet impact in AD536?". *Astronomy and Geophysics* 45 (1): 1.23. Accessed online 30 August 2012 at <http://onlinelibrary.wiley.com/doi/10.1046/j.1468-4004.2003.45123.x/abstract>.

[130] Finsinger, Walter and Willy Tinner. "Holocene vegetation and land use changes in response to climatic changes in the forelands of the southwestern Alps, Italy." *Journal of Quaternary Science.* Wiley InterScience. 2006: Vol. 1, pp. 243-258. Accessed online 16 August 2012 at <http://igitur-archive.library.uu.nl/bio/2008-0930-200335/Finsinger_06_ Holocene vegetation.pdf>.

[131] LaViolette, Paul. "A Galactic Superwave Hazard Alert Update." Starbust Foundation. August 2009. Accessed online 3 September 2012 at <http://www.starburstfound.org/downloads/superwave/Nexus2009.pdf>.

[132] Napier, W.M. "Comets, Catastrophes, and Earth's History." *Journal of Cosmology*, 2009, Vol 2, pages 344-355. Accessed online 31 August 2012 at <http://journalofcosmology.com/Extinction117.html>.

[133] Van Stone, Mark. "What happened at the last 13.0.0.0.0 Creation…" 2012Part2. FAMSI. Accessed online 26 Nov 2010 at <http://www.famsi.org/research/vanstone/2012/2012Part2.pdf>.

[134] "Mayan Zodiac." Xcaret Magazine Mexico. Accessed online 18 March 2010 at <http://www.xcaretmagazine.com/xcaret-ll/mayan-zodiac.php>.

[135] Zender, Marc. "The Raccoon Glyph in Classic Maya Writing." *The PARI Journal*. The Precolumbian Art Research Institute. Spring 2005: Volume V, Number 4. Accessed online 16 August 2012 at <http://www.mesoweb.com/pari/journal/archive/PARI0504.pdf>.

[136] Sagan, Carl. *Comet.*

[137] Vaquero, J.M. "Historical Sunspot Observation: A Review." Arxiv.org. Accessed online 18 August 2012 at <http://arxiv.org/pdf/astro-ph/0702068.pdf>.

[138] Vaquero, J.M. "Historical Sunspot Observation: A Review." Arxiv.org. Accessed online 18 August 2012 at <http://arxiv.org/pdf/astro-ph/0702068.pdf>.

[139] Carrington, R. C. "Description of a Singular Appearance seen in the Sun on September 1, 1859". *Monthly Notices of the Royal Astronomical Society.* 1859: 20, 13–5.
[140] "Solar Storm of 1859." Wikipedia.org. Accessed online 13 September 2012 at <http://en.wikipedia.org/wiki/Solar_storm_of_1859>.
[141] Kobres, Bob. "Comets and the Bronze Age Collapse." Accessed online 11 September 2012 at <http://abob.libs.uga.edu/bobk/bronze.html>.
[142] Kobres, Bob. "Comets and the Bronze Age Collapse." Accessed online 11 September 2012 at <http://abob.libs.uga.edu/bobk/bronze.html>.
[143] "Rahu and Ketu - A study in Vedic Mantra." Astrobix.com. Accessed online 12 September 2012 at <http://astrobix.com/learn/250-rahu-and-ketu-a-study-in-vedic-mantra.html>.
[144] "Rahu." Wikipedia.org. Accessed online 12 September 2012 at <http://en.wikipedia.org/wiki/Rahu>.
[145] "Sudarshana Chakra." Wikipedia.org. Accessed online 13 September 2012 at <http://en.wikipedia.org/wiki/Sudarshana_Chakra>.
[146] "Rahu." Wikipedia.org. Accessed online 24 October 2012 at <http://en.wikipedia.org/wiki/Rahu>.
[147] Andrews, Munya. *The Seven Sisters of the Pleiades: Stories from Around the World.* Spinifex Press, 2005. Accessed online 24 September 2012 at <http://books.google.com/books?id=YwGEo50bla8C&lpg=PA41&ots=uBQeib_3Fu&dq=honeybees, honeycombs bee goddesses&pg=PA41 - v=onepage&q=honeybees, honeycombs bee goddesses&f=false>.
[148] Garcia, Erik Velasquez. "The Maya Flood Myth and the Decapitation of the Cosmic Caiman." PARI Online Publications. Accessed online 24 September 2012 at <http://www.mesoweb.com/pari/publications/journal/701/flood_e.pdf>.
[149] "Gorgon." Wikipedia.org. Accessed online 20 September 2012 at <http://en.wikipedia.org/wiki/Gorgon>.

[150] Blakeslee, Sandra. "Epic Crash, Ancient Wave." NYTimes.com. 14 November 2006. Accessed online 20 September 2012 at <http://www.nytimes.com/2006/11/14/science/14WAVE.html?_r=0>.

[151] Abbott, Dallas. "Burckle Abyssal Impact Crater: Did this Impact Produce a Global Deluge?" Accessed online 20 September 2012 at <http://www.earth2class.org/k12/w8_s2007/CRBurckleAbyssalImpactCra%5B1%5D.htm>.

[152] "Tlaltecuhtli." Wikipedia.org. Accessed online 20 September 2012 at <http://en.wikipedia.org/wiki/Tlaltecuhtli>.

[153] Kaufman, David. "Did Ancient China Influence Olmec Mexico?" Academia.edu. Accessed online 31 October 2012 at <http://www.academia.edu/867576/Did_Ancient_China_Influence_Olmec_Mexico>.

[154] "Taotie." Wikipedia.org. Accessed online 31 October 2012 at <http://en.wikipedia.org/wiki/Taotie>.

[155] "Taotie." Wikipedia.org. Accessed online 31 October 2012 at <http://en.wikipedia.org/wiki/Taotie>.

[156] Kaufman, David. "Did Ancient China Influence Olmec Mexico?" Academia.edu. Accessed online 31 October 2012 at <http://www.academia.edu/867576/Did_Ancient_China_Influence_Olmec_Mexico>.

[157] Meggers, Betty J. 1975. "The Transpacific Origin of Mesoamerican Civilization: A Preliminary Review of the Evidence and Its Theoretical Implications." In *American Anthropologist*, Vol. 77, No. 1, pp. 1-27.

[158] Stirling, Matthew W. "Early history of the olmec problem." Dumbarton Oaks Conference on the Olmecs. Accessed online 31 October 2012 at <http://www.doaks.org/resources/publications/doaks_online_publications/Olmec.pdf>.

[159] Fenyvesi, Charles. "A Tale of Two Cultures: A Beijing Scholar Links an Ancient Chinese Dynasty to the New World's Earliest Civilization." *U.S. News and World Report*, November 4, 1996, pp. 46-48.

[160] Xu, Mike. "Transpacific Contacts?" TCU.edu. Accessed online 31 October 2012 at <http://www.chinese.tcu.edu/www_chinese3_tcu_edu.htm>.

[161] Stross, Brian. "Some Observations on T585 (Quincunx) of the Maya Script." UTexas.edu. Accessed online 31 October 2012 at <http://www.utexas.edu/courses/stross/papers/quin.rtf>.

[162] Stross, Brian. "Some Observations on T585 (Quincunx) of the Maya Script." UTexas.edu. Accessed online 31 October 2012 at <http://www.utexas.edu/courses/stross/papers/quin.rtf>.

[163] Stross, Brian. "Some Observations on T585 (Quincunx) of the Maya Script." UTexas.edu. Accessed online 31 October 2012 at <http://www.utexas.edu/courses/stross/papers/quin.rtf>.

[164] "Tarim Mummies." Wikipedia.org. Accessed online 24 October 2012 at < http://en.wikipedia.org/wiki/Tarim_mummies>.

[165] Mair, Victor H., "Mummies of the Tarim Basin," *Archaeology*, vol. 48, no. 2, pages 28–35 (March/April 1995).

[166] "Viracocha." Wikipedia.org. Accessed online 25 October 2012 at <http://en.wikipedia.org/wiki/Viracocha>.

[167] "Bochica." Wikipedia.org. Accessed online 25 October 2012 at < http://en.wikipedia.org/wiki/Bochica>.

[168] Marsh, Peter. "Genetics Rewrites Pacific Prehistory." *Polynesian Pathways*. Accessed online 28 October 2012 at <http://users.on.net/~mkfenn/GeneticsrewritesPacificprehistory.htm>.

[169] Schock, Robert. "The Mystery of Gobekli Tepe and Its Message to Us." *New Dawn Magazine*. September 2010. Accessed online 28 October 2012 at <http://www.robertschoch.com/articles/schochgobeklitepenewdawnsept2010.pdf>.

[170] Kelley, David B. "Cultural Diffusion." 1997. Accessed online 24 October 2012 at <http://mysite.verizon.net/vzeu87dp/id2.html>.

[171] Kelley, David B. "Cultural Diffusion." 1997. Accessed online 24 October 2012 at <http://mysite.verizon.net/vzeu87dp/id2.html>.

[172] Bryner, Jeanna. "One Common Ancestor Behind Blue Eyes." LiveScience.com. January 21, 2008. Accessed online 25 October 2012 at <http://www.livescience.com/9578-common-ancestor-blue-eyes.html>.

[173] Ingram, James (trans). "Anglo-Saxon Chronicles" Accessed online 24 November 2010 at <http://classiclit.about.com/library/bl-etexts/anon/bl-anon-anglo-saxon-3.htm>.
[174] Abbott, Dallas. "Exotic Grains in a Core from Cornwall, NY- Do They Have an Impact Source?" Journal of Siberian Federal University. Accessed online 24 September 2012 at <http://www.scribd.com/doc/61276495/Exotic-Grains-in-a-Core-From-Cornwall-NY-Do-They-Have-an-Impact-Source>.
[175] Culver, Stephen J, et al. "Late Holocene Barrier Island Collapse: Outer Banks, North Carolina, USA." *The Sedimentary Record*. Society for Sedementary Geology, December 2007: pp. 4-8. Accessed online 18 July 2012 at <http://www.scribd.com/doc/77171096/North-Carolina-Tsunami>.
[176] Howard, George. "Hurricane or Tsunami?: North Carolina coast turns to Tar Hell around time of Magna Carta." CosmicTusk.com. Accessed online 17 July 2012 at <http://cosmictusk.com/hurricane-or-tsunami-north-carolina-coast-turns-to-tar-hell-around-time-of-battle-of-hastings/>.
[177] Astapovič, I. S., and Terenteva, A. K. In *Physics and Dynamics of Meteors*.
Kresák, L., and Millman, P. M (Eds.). IAU Symposium 33. Reidel, Dordrecht.
1968. p. 308.
[178] Jenkins, John Major. *Maya Cosmogenesis 2012*.
[179] Aveni, Anthony. "Astronomical considerations in the Aztec expression of history: Eclipse data." *Ancient Mesoamerica*, 10 (1999), 87-98. Accessed online 26 Nov 2010 at <http://www.mexicauprising.net/aztececlipsedata.pdf>.
[180] Umberger, Emily. "The Structure of Aztec History." *Archaeoastronomy, The Bulletin of the Center for Archaeoastronomy* IV (1981):10-18.
[181] Aveni, Anthony. "Astronomical considerations in the aztec expression of history: Eclipse data." *Ancient Mesoamerica*, 10 (1999), 87-98. Accessed online 26 Nov 2010 at <http://www.mexicauprising.net/aztececlipsedata.pdf>.

[182] "Huitzilopochtli." Wikipedia.org. Accessed online 18 July 2012 at <http://en.wikipedia.org/wiki/Huitzilopochtli>.

[183] Townsend, Richard F. *State and Cosmos in the Art of Tenochtitlan*. p.70 Accessed online 26 Nov 2010 at <http://books.google.com/books?id=Xn-lIHpVG7oC&lpg=PP1&ots=TbZDDrTW11&dq=richard f. townsend&pg=PA70 - v=onepage&q&f=false>.

[184] Van Stone, Mark. "So, Is Our World Going to End in 2012?" *2012: Science and Prophecy of the Ancient Maya (Four Page Flyer)*.

[185] Stuart, David. "More on Tortuguero's Monument 6 and the Prophecy that Wasn't." *Maya Decipherment*. 4 October 2011. Accessed online 22 September 2012 at <http://decipherment.wordpress.com/2011/10/04/more-on-tortugueros-monument-6-and-the-prophecy-that-wasnt/>.

[186] Gronemeyer, Sven and Barbara MacCleod. "What could happen in 2012?" *Wayeb Notes*. Wayeb.org. Accessed online 22 September 2012 at <http://www.wayeb.org/notes/wayeb_notes0034.pdf>.

[187] Grofe, Michael J. "The Name of God L: Bolon Yokte Kuh?" *Wayeb Notes*. Accessed online 22 September 2012 at <http://www.wayeb.org/notes/wayeb_notes0030.pdf>.

[188] Bolles, David and Alejandra. "World Creation Stories from Kom Cheen, Yucatan." *A Grammar of the Yucatecan Mayan Language*. FAMSI.org. Accessed online 22 September 2012 at <http://www.famsi.org/research/bolles/grammar/section41.htm>.

[189] Gronemeyer, Sven and Barbara MacCleod. "What could happen in 2012?" *Wayeb Notes*. Wayeb.org. Accessed online 22 September 2012 at <http://www.wayeb.org/notes/wayeb_notes0034.pdf>.

[190] "Comet Swift-Tuttle." Wikipedia.org. Accessed online 24 September 2012 at <http://en.wikipedia.org/wiki/Comet_Swift-Tuttle>.

[191] "Yule goat." Wikipedia.org. Accessed online 26 October 2012 at <http://en.wikipedia.org/wiki/Yule_goat>.

[192] "Cosmic Explosion Among the Brightest in Recorded History." NASA.gov. Accessed online 26 October 2012 at

<http://www.nasa.gov/vision/universe/watchtheskies/swift_nsu_02 05.html>.

[193] "2004 Indian Ocean tsunami bulletins." Wikisource.org. Accessed online 26 October 2012 at <http://en.wikisource.org/wiki/2004_Indian_Ocean_tsunami_bulletins#December_25.2C_2004>.

About the Author

Gary C. Daniels has had a lifelong interest in Native American and Mesoamerican culture. He is a writer, television producer and documentary filmmaker and began seriously researching these cultures in 2001 while pursuing his Master's Degree in Communications at Georgia State University in Atlanta. This research culminated in the production of a documentary film, Lost Worlds: Georgia and website, LostWorlds.org.

During this research he noticed that many Native American civilizations in the Southeastern U.S. lasted for around 250 years before collapsing. Later he learned of the Maya belief in a 256-year *katun* cycle that governed the rise and fall of civilizations. Intrigued he delved deeper into Maya beliefs immersing himself in their mythology and religious beliefs finding many similarities between the cultures of the Southeastern U.S. and Mesoamerica as well as the possible presence of Maya in America. It was then that he discovered their "prophecies" related to this 256-year *katun* cycle. His research resulted in the creation of the websites 2012Quest.com and MayaProphecies.com.

He is currently working on a new book entitled *Maya In America* that reveals the extent of the Maya influence and presence in North America. You can learn more at http://www.MayaInAmerica.com

He is also researching a second book on the Mayan prophecies entitled The Real Mayan Prophecies which brings together his latest findings and research on Maya history, mythology, religion and predictions about the future. Learn more at http://TheRealMayanProphecies.com

Printed in Great Britain
by Amazon